RUSSIAN LITERATURE
THEATRE AND ART

RUSSIAN LITERATURE THEATRE AND ART

A Bibliography of works in
English, published 1900–1945

by

AMREI ETTLINGER, Ph.D.
JOAN M. GLADSTONE, B.A. (Lond.)

KENNIKAT PRESS
Port Washington, N. Y./London

RUSSIAN LITERATURE, THEATRE AND ART

First published in 1945
Reissued in 1971 by Kennikat Press
Library of Congress Catalog Card No: 72-118410
ISBN 0-8046-1187-4

Manufactured by Taylor Publishing Company   Dallas, Texas

PREFACE

THE following bibliography is designed to serve two purposes. We wanted to make the approach to Russian and Soviet literature easier for the general reader, and to provide at the same time a basis for serious research work in the literary field.

The bibliography, which does not claim to be completely exhaustive, has been limited to books and pamphlets published between 1900 and 1945. As it is concerned mainly with Russian and Soviet literature and kindred subjects, the material had to be restricted, and many aspects of Russian and Soviet culture, such as music, had to be left out. Our object has been to supplement Mr. P. Grierson's admirable compilation, *Books on Soviet Russia, 1917–42*, published in 1943, to which we would refer all readers who are looking for information on the political, sociological and historical life of Russia. There is room for a future publication to cover the period before 1900, and a host of material in periodicals. Articles in periodicals are quoted here only when reference seemed absolutely necessary.

As to the practical use of the bibliography, we hope that the material is arranged clearly enough for finding items quickly. Round brackets designate the name of the series in which a book has been published, or may contain the abbreviation of a title which has been quoted before in full. Square brackets are used for more detailed information about the character of a book, particularly in the case of collections. In the section "Individual Russian Authors", collected works are noted before separate works.

For transliteration, the scheme of the Washington Library of Congress has been followed with certain modifications.

Owing to war conditions, not all the books mentioned have been available, and in a number of cases it has not been possible to verify details of contents, etc.

Our warmest thanks for untiring interest and constant help are due to Dr. W. Bonser, Professor J. Lavrin, and last, but not least, to Professor S. Konovalov.

AMREI ETTLINGER.
JOAN M. GLADSTONE.

December, 1945.

CONTENTS

ABBREVIATIONS

anon.	anonymous(ly).
c.	circa.
comp.	compiled.
cont.	continued.
ed.	edition, edited.
Engl.	English.
ibid.	ibidem.
ill.	illustrated.
incl.	including.
Ld.	London.
ltd.	limited.
n.d.	no date.
N.Y.	New York.
Oxf.	Oxford.
pl.	plates.
pp.	pages.
pseud.	pseudonym.
pt.	part.
repr.	reprint(ed).
rev.	revised.
transl.	translation, translated.
Univ. Pr.	University Press.
U.S.A.	for : published in the United States, publisher unknown.
VOKS.	Soviet Union Society for Cultural Relations with Foreign Countries.
vol(s).	volume(s).

I. GENERAL BIBLIOGRAPHY

BAKER (E. A.) and PACKMAN (J.): *A guide to the best fiction,* Engl. and American, incl. transl. from foreign languages. New ed. 634 pp. Ld. Routledge, 1932.

BRISTOL PUBLIC LIBRARY: *Russia, a select reading list.* 27 pp. Bristol, 1942.

CAMPBELL (J. M.): *Selected list of Russian books*; comp. for the Free Public Library Commission of Massachusetts. (Foreign book list, 7.) N.Y. 1916.

Commercial Year Book of the Soviet Union. See: Soviet Union Year Book.

DOMINCOVICH (H. A.): *Russian literature for the Engl. classroom.* Engl. Journal, December, 1942.

GRIERSON (P.): *Books on Soviet Russia, 1917–1942*; a bibliography and a guide to reading. 354 pp. Ld. Methuen, 1943.

KERNER (R. J.): *Slavic Europe*; a selected bibliography in the Western European languages, comprising history, languages and literatures. (Harvard Bibliographies. Library series, 1.) 402 pp. Cambridge, Mass. Harvard Univ. Pr., 1918.

MARTIANOFF (N. N.): *Books available in Engl. by Russians and on Russia.* 4th ed. 48 pp. N.Y. Martianoff, 1942.

MARTIANOFF (N. N.) and STERN (M. A.): *Almanac of Russian artists in America.* 249 pp. Ill. N.Y. Martinanoff, 1932.

MOHRENSCHILDT (S. von): *Books in Engl. on Russian literature, 1917–42.* Russian Review, autumn 1942.

Soviet Union Year Book, 1930. Comp. and ed. by A. A. Santalov and L. Segal. 670 pp. Ld. Allen & Unwin, 1930. [Contains: Who's Who in literature.]

U.S.S.R. Handbook. 643 pp. Ld. Gollancz, 1936. [Contains: a chapter on literature, and a Who's Who.]

WRIGHT (C. T. H.): *A classified list of books relating to Russia and Russian affairs,* mostly published in England since 1910. 23 pp. 1917.

II. STUDIES IN RUSSIAN LITERATURE

GENERAL WORKS

BARING (M.): *Landmarks in Russian literature.* 299 pp. 3rd ed. Ld. Methuen, 1916.
—— *The mainsprings of Russia.* 328 pp. Ld. Nelson, 1914.
—— *An outline of Russian literature.* 256 pp. Ld. Williams & Norgate, 1915. 2nd ed. Oxf. Univ. Pr., 1928. Repr. Thornton Butterworth, 1929. (Home university library.)
—— *Russian essays and stories.* 295 pp. Ld. Methuen, 1908.
—— *The Russian people.* 366 pp. Ld. Methuen, 1911.
BOWRA (C. M.): *The heritage of symbolism.* 340 pp. N.Y. Macmillan, 1943. [Contains : chapter on Blok.] 244 pp. Ld. Macmillan, 1943.
BRASOL (B. L.): *The mighty three : Pushkin, Gogol, Dostoevsky.* A critical trilogy, with an introduction by C. A. Manning. 295 pp. N.Y. and Ld. Williams & Norgate, 1937.
BRUECKNER (A.): *A literary history of Russia.* Ed. by E. H. Minns. Transl. from the German by H. Havelock. (Library of literary history, 9.) 558 pp. Ld. Fisher Unwin, 1908.
CHADWICK (H. M.) and CHADWICK (N. K.): *Growth of literature,* II, pt. 1: Russian oral literature, pp. 1–298. Cambridge Univ. Pr., 1936.
EASTMAN (M.): *Art and the life of action ; with other essays.* 189 pp. Ld. Allen, 1935.
—— *Artists in uniform: a study of literature and bureaucratism.* 261 pp. Ld. Allen & Unwin, 1934.
ELTON (O.): *Essays and addresses.* 275 pp. N.Y. Longmans, 1939. [Incl. essays on Pushkin and Chekhov.]
FLORES (A.) ed.: *Literature and Marxism*; a controversy by Soviet critics. (Critics group series, 9.) 95 pp. N.Y. Critics Group, 1938.
GUTHRIE (A. L.): *Russian literature ; a study outline.* 53 pp. N.Y., 1917.
HAPGOOD (I. F.): *A survey of Russian literature,* with selections. 279 pp. N.Y. Chautauqua Pr., 1902.

10

HUTTON (J. A.): *Guidance on Russia from her literature.* 169 pp. Ld. Hodder & Stoughton, 1930.

KAUN (A. S.) and SIMMONS (E. J.) ed.: *Slavic studies*; 16 essays in honour of G. R. Noyes. 242 pp. Ithaca, Cornell Univ. Pr., 1943.

KROPOTKIN (Prince P. A.): *Russian literature.* 341 pp. N.Y. McClure, Phillips, 1905.
　　With title: *Russian literature, ideals and realities.* 341 pp. Ld. Duckworth, 1915.

KUNITZ (J.): *Russian literature and the Jew ; a sociological inquiry into the nature and origin of literary patterns.* 195 pp. N.Y. Columbia Univ. Pr., 1929.

LAVRIN (J.): *Studies in European literature.* 222 pp. Ld. Constable, 1929. [Essays on: Turgenev; Tolstoy and Nietzsche; Chekhov and Maupassant; Dostoevsky and Proust.]

—— *Aspects of modernism: from Wilde to Pirandello.* 247 pp. Ld. Nott, 1936. [Incl. essays on: Blok, Esenin, Rozanov.]

—— *Russian literature.* 80 pp. (Benn's sixpenny library.) Ld. Benn, 1927.

MACKIEWICZ (M. N.): *Russian minds in fetters.* 184 pp. Ld. Allen & Unwin, 1932.

MAIS (S. P. B.): *Why we should read.* 311 pp. N.Y. Dodd, Mead & Co, 1921. [Incl. essays on: Chekhov, Dostoevsky, Gogol, Goncharov, Lermontov, Nekrasov, Pushkin, Tolstoy, Turgenev.]

MANNING (C. A.): *Ukrainian literature ; studies of the leading authors.* 126 pp. N.Y. Ukrainian Nat. Association, 1944.

MASARYK (T. G.): *The spirit of Russia ; studies in history, literature and philosophy.* Transl. by E. and C. Paul. 2 vols. 480, 585 pp. Ld. Allen & Unwin, 1919.

MILIUKOV (P. N.): *Outlines of Russian culture.* Ed. by M. M. Karpovich. Transl. by V. Ughet and E. Davis. 3 pts. (Pt. 2: Literature.) 126 pp. Philadelphia. Univ. of Pennsylvania Pr., 1942.

MIRSKY (Prince D. S.): *Contemporary Russian literature, 1881–1925.* (Contemporary literature series.) 372 pp. Ld. Routledge, 1933.

—— *A history of Russian literature from the earliest times to the death of Dostoevsky* (1881). 388 pp. Ld. Routledge, 1927.

—— *Modern Russian literature.* 120 pp. (The world's manuals). Ld. Oxf. Univ. Pr., 1925.

New Directions in prose and poetry, 1941. Ed. by J. Laughlin. 729 pp. Norfolk, Conn. New Directions, 1941. [Contains: pp. 515–650. Soviet Russian poetry, a survey, translations and critical essays.]

OLGIN (M. J.) : *A guide to Russian literature (1820–1917)*. 323 pp. Ld. Cape, 1921. [Contains translated ext·acts from Russian critics, a commentary by Olgin and analysis of selected works.]

SEGAL (L.) : *The romantic movement in Russia*. 91 pp. Portsmouth, 1922.

SIMMONS (E. J.) : *English literature and culture in Russia (1553–1840)*. 357 pp. (Harvard studies in comparative literature, 12.) Cambridge, Mass. Harvard Univ. Pr., 1935.

—— *Outline of modern Russian literature, 1880–1940*. 93 pp. Ithaca. Cornell Univ. Pr., 1943.

SHAKNOVSKY : *A short history of Russian literature*. Transl. with a supplementary chapter by S. Tomkeyeff. 180 pp. Ld. Kegan Paul, 1921.

SOVIET WRITERS' CONGRESS, 1934 : Problems of Soviet literature ; reports and speeches at the First Soviet Writers' Congress, by A. A. Zhdanov and others. Ed. by H. G. Scott. 279 pp. N.Y. International Publishers, 1935. Ld. Lawrence, 1936.

STEPHENS (W.) : *The soul of Russia*. 307 pp. Ld. Macmillan, 1916.

STRUVE (G.) : *Soviet Russian literature*. 270 pp. Ld. Routledge, 1935.

—— *25 years of Soviet Russian literature, 1918–1943*. New ed. of : *Soviet Russian literature*. 347 pp. Ld. Routledge, 1944.

U.S.S.R. speaks for itself. 4 pts. (in 1). Pt. 4 : *Culture and leisure*. Ld. Lawrence & Wishart, 1943.

VOYNICH (E. L.) : *The humour of Russia*. Ld. Scott, 1911. [With specimens.]

WALISZEWSKI (K.) : *A history of Russian literature*. 450 pp. (Short histories of the literatures of the world, 8.) Ld. Heinemann, 1900 ; Appleton, 1927.

WIENER (L.) : *Aṅ interpretation of the Russian people*. 248 pp. N.Y. McBride, 1915.

WILLIAMS (H. W.) : *Russia of the Russians*. 430 pp. Ld. Pitman, 1914. Repr. 1920. [Contains chapters on the press, literature, theatre.]

WOOLF (V.) : *The Russian point of view*. (*In* : The common reader. Ld. Hogarth Pr., 1925.)

YARMOLINSKY (A.) : *Russian literature*. 56 pp. (Reading with a purpose, 61.) Chicago. American Library Association, 1931.

POETRY

JARINTZOV (N.) : *Russian poets and poems: classics and moderns.*
With an introduction on Russian versification. Vol. I:
Classics. 357 pp. Oxf. Blackwell, 1917. [Only vol. I seems
to have been published.]

KAUN (A. S.) : *Soviet poets and poetry.* 208 pp. Berkeley. Univ.
of California Pr., 1943.

NEWMARCH (R. H.): *Poetry and progress.* Ld. Lane, 1907.

PATRICK (G. Z.): *Popular poetry in Soviet Russia.* 289 pp.
Berkeley. Univ. of California Pr., 1929. [Account of post-
revolutionary peasant poetry, with transl.]

ZNAKOMY (L.) and LEVIN (D.): *A decade of Soviet poetry.* (*In:*
New Directions in prose and poetry, 1941, pp. 621-27.)

THE NOVEL

LAVRIN (J.): *An introduction to the Russian novel.* 216 pp. Ld.
Methuen, 1942.

MIRSKY (Prince D. S.): *See:* WALPOLE (H.) and others: *Ten-*
dencies of the modern novel.

PERSKY (S.): *Contemporary Russian novelists.* Transl. from the
French by F. Eisemann. 317 pp. 2nd ed. Ld. Palmer, 1915.

PHELPS (W. L.): *Essays on Russian novelists.* With a bibliography by A. Keogh. 322 pp. N.Y. Macmillan, 1911.

VOGÜÉ (E. M. M., vicomte de): *The Russian novel.* Transl. from
the 11th French ed. by H. A. Sawyer. 337 pp. Ld. Chapman & Hall, 1913; N.Y. 1916.

WALPOLE (H.) and others: *Tendencies of the modern novel.* Ill.
160 pp. Ld. Allen & Unwin, 1934. [Contains: MIRSKY
(Prince D. S.): *The Soviet Russian novel.*]

III. STUDIES IN RUSSIAN THEATRE AND ART

DRAMA, THEATRE, FILM

AROSSEV (A.) comp.: *Soviet cinema; a compilation by many authors.* 312 pp. Moscow. VOKS, 1935.

BAKSHY (A.): *The path of the modern Russian stage, and other essays.* Ld. Palmer & Haywood, 1916.

BATES (A.): *Russian drama.* Ld. Historical Publishing Co., 1906.

BROWN (B. W.): *Theatre at the left.* 105 pp. U.S.A. Booke shop, 1938.

BRYHER, pseud.: *Film problems of Soviet Russia.* 140 pp. Ld. Territet, 1929.

CARTER (H.): *The new spirit in the European theatre, 1914–1924 ; a comparative study of the changes effected by war and revolution.* 292 pp. Ld. Benn, 1925.

―― *The new spirit in the Russian theatre, 1917–1928, and a sketch of the Russian cinema and radio.* Pl. 348 pp. N.Y. Brentano's; Ld. Shaylor, 1929.

―― *The new theatre and cinema of Soviet Russia.* 278 pp. Ld. Chapman & Dadd, 1924.

CHANDLER (F. W.): *Aspects of modern drama.* N.Y. Macmillan, 1918.

―― *Modern continental playwrights.* (Plays and playwrights series.) 711 pp. N.Y. and Ld. Harper, 1931. [Contains: bibl. of Russian authors in Engl.]

CHARQUES (R. D.) ed.: *Footnotes to the theatre.* Pl. 335 pp. Ld. Davies, 1939.

CLARK (B. H.): *A study of modern drama ; a handbook . . . of the last three quarters of a century.* Rev. ed. 534 pp. N.Y. and Ld. Appleton, 1938.

COLEMAN (A. P.): *Humour in the Russian comedy from Catherine to Gogol.* (Columbia Univ. Slavonic studies, vol. 2.) 92 pp. N.Y. Columbia Univ. Pr., 1925.

DANA (H. W. L.): *Drama in wartime Russia.* N.Y. National Council of American-Soviet Friendship, 1943.

14

—— *Handbook on Soviet drama : lists of theatres, plays, operas, ballets, films, and books and articles about them.* 158 pp. N.Y. American Russian Institute, 1938.

DICKINSON (T. H.) and others : *The theatre in a changing Europe.* 492 pp. Ld. Putnam, 1938. [Contains: The Russian theatre, by J. Gregor and H. W. L. Dana.]

EFIMOVA (N. Y.) : *Adventures of a Russian puppet theatre.* Transl. by E. Mitcoff. 199 pp. Birmingham, Michigan. McPharlin, 1935.

EISENSTEIN (S. M.) : *The film sense.* Transl. by J. Leyda. 207 pp. Ld. Faber, 1943.

FLANAGAN (H.) : *Shifting scenes of the modern European theatre.* Pl. 280 pp. Ld. Harrap, 1929.

FOVITSKY (A. L.) : *Moscow Art Theatre and its distinguishing characteristics.* Ill. 48 pp. N.Y. Chernoff, 1922.

FÜLÖP-MILLER (R.) and GREGOR (J.) : *Mind and face of Bolshevism, an examination of cultural life in Soviet Russia.* Transl. by F. S. Flint and D. F. Tait. 308 pp. Ld. Putnam, 1927.

—— *The Russian theatre, its character and history, with special reference to the revolutionary period.* Transl. by P. England. Ill. 136 pp. Philadelphia. Lippincott; Ld. Harrap, 1930.

GRIFFITH (H. F.) ed.: *Playtime in Russia,* by various authors. Ill. 249 pp. Ld. Methuen, 1935.

GYSEGHEM (A. van) : *Theatre in Soviet Russia.* Ill. 220 pp. Ld. Faber, 1943.

HOUGHTON (N.) : *Moscow rehearsals : an account of methods of production in the Soviet theatre.* Ill. 291 pp. N.Y. Harcourt Brace, 1936.

—— Slightly different ed. 313 pp. Ld. G. Allen, 1938.

KOMMISSARZHEVSKY (F. F.) : *Costume of the theatre.* 178 pp. Ld. Bles, 1931.

—— *Myself and the theatre.* Ill. 205 pp. Ld. Heinemann, 1929.

LONDON (K.) : *The seven Soviet arts.* Transl. by E. Bensinger. Ill. 382 pp. Ld. Faber, 1937 : N.Y. Yale Univ. Pr., 1938.

MACLEOD (J.) : *The new Soviet theatre.* Ill. 242 pp. Ld. Allen & Unwin, 1943.

MARKOV (P. A.) : *The Soviet theatre.* (New Soviet library, 3.) 176 pp. Ld. Gollancz, 1934.

MOSCOW THEATRE FOR CHILDREN : *An album of photographs illustrating the work of the oldest professional theatre for children.* 96 pp. Ld. M. Lawrence, 1934.

NEMIROVICH—DANCHENKO (V. I.) : *My life in the Russian theatre.* Transl. by J. Cournos. 358 pp. Ld. Bles, 1936.

NILSEN (V. S.): *The cinema as a graphic art ; on a theory of representation in the cinema.* With an appreciation by S. M. Eisenstein. Transl. by S. Garry. Ill. 227 pp. Ld. Newnes, 1937.

PERRY (H. ten Eyck): *Masters of dramatic comedy and their social themes.* 428 pp. Cambridge, Mass. Harvard Univ. Pr., 1939.

PUDOVKIN (V. I.): *Film acting : a course of lectures delivered at the State Institute of Cinematography, Moscow.* Transl. by I. Montagu. (Filmcraft series.) 153 pp. Ld. Newnes, 1935.

—— *Film technique : 5 essays and 2 addresses.* Transl. and annotated by I. Montagu. (Filmcraft series.) 204 pp. Ld. Newnes, 1933.

ROTHA (P.): *The film till now ; a survey of the cinema.* 362 pp. Ld. Cape, 1930.

—— *Movie parade.* 142 pp. Ld. Studio, 1936.

SAYLER (O. M.): *Inside the Moscow Art Theatre.* Ill. 240 pp. N.Y. Brentano's, 1925; Ld. Brentano's, 1928.

—— *Russian players in America.* (Etched text and pictures.) Ltd. ed. U.S.A. Wall, 1923.

—— *Russian theatre under the revolution.* 273 pp. Boston. Little, Brown, 1920.

—— *Russian theatre.* 364 pp. Ld. and N.Y. Brentano's, 1922. [Enlarged ed. of above.]

SHALIAPIN (F. I.): *Pages from my life ; an autobiography.* Transl. by H. M. Buck. Rev. and enlarged ed. by K. Wright. 345 pp. N.Y. Harper, 1927.

—— With title : *Man and mask ; forty years in the life of a singer.* Transl. P. Mégroz. 413 pp. Ld. Gollancz, 1932.

SMIRNOV (A. A.): *Shakespeare : a Marxist interpretation.* Transl. by S. Volochova and others : special ed. for the New Theatre League. (Critics group series, 2.) 95 pp. N.Y. Critics Group, 1936.

STANISLAVSKY (K.) [pseud. of K. S. Alekseev]: *An actor prepares.* Transl. by E. R. Hapgood. 313 pp. Ld. Bles, 1936.

—— *My life in art.* Transl. by J. J. Robbins. 586 pp. Ld. Bles, 1924.

The theatre in the U.S.S.R. Published by the Soviet Union Society for Cultural Relations with Foreign Countries. (VOKS), vol. 6. Ill. 108 pp. Moscow, 1934.

VOLKOV (N.): *Moscow theatre.* Issued in English by Intourist for the second annual theatre festival. 86 pp. Moscow, 1934.

WEIR (A. E.): *Thesaurus of the arts: drama, music . . . painting, screen . . . literature, sculpture, architecture, ballet.* N.Y. 1943.

WIENER (L.): *Contemporary drama of Russia.* (Contemporary drama series.) N.Y. Little, 1924.

ZELIKSON (M.) comp.: *The artist of the Kamerni theatre: 1914–1934.* Ill. 212 pp. Moscow, 1935.

BALLET

AMBROSE (K.): *Ballet-lovers' pocket book.* 64 pp. Ld. Black, 1943.

ANTHONY (G.): *Massine. See:* MASSINE.

—— *Russian ballet; camera studies.* With an introduction by A. Haskell. Ltd. ed. Pl. 32 pp. Ld. Bles, 1939.

Ballet Russe; the heart of ballet music. Ill. 96 pp. N.Y., c. 1942.

BEAUMONT (C. W.): *Complete book of ballets; a guide to the principal ballets of the 19th and 20th century.* Pl. 900 pp. Ld. Putnam, 1938.

—— *Design for the ballet.* Ed. by C. G. Holme. Special winter number of the *Studio.* 152 pp. Ld. Studio Ltd., 1937.

—— New rev. ed. 156 pp. Ld. Studio, 1939.

—— *Diaghilev. See:* DIAGHILEV (S.).

—— *The Diaghilev ballet. See:* DIAGHILEV (S.).

—— *Five centuries of ballet design.* Pl. 136 pp. Ld. Studio Ltd., 1939.

—— *Fokine. See:* FOKINE (M.)

—— *A history of ballet in Russia, 1613–1881.* Pl. 140 pp. Ld. Beaumont, 1930.

—— *Nijinsky. See:* NIJINSKY (V.).

—— *Pavlova. See:* PAVLOVA (A.).

—— *Short history of ballet.* Pl. (Essays on dancing and dancers, 4.) 40 pp. Ld. Beaumont, 1933.

—— *Supplement to Complete book of ballets.* Pl. 208 pp. Ld. Beaumont, 1942.

BENOIS (A.): *Reminiscences of the Russian ballet.* Transl. by M. Britnieva. Pl. 414 pp. Ld. Putnam, 1941.

BOURMAN (A.) and LYMAN (D.): *The tragedy of Nijinsky. See:* NIJINSKY (V.).

DANDRÉ (V. E.): *Anna Pavlova. See:* PAVLOVA (A.).

DIAGHILEV (S.) :

—— BEAUMONT (C. W.) : *The Diaghilev ballet in London ; a personal record.* 355 pp. Ld. Putnam, 1940.

—— BEAUMONT (C. W.) : *Sergei Diaghilev.* Pl. (Essays on dancing and dancers, 3.) 28 pp. Ld. Beaumont, 1933.

—— HASKELL (A. L.) and NOUVEL (W.) : *Diaghileff: his artistic and private life.* Pl. 359 pp. Ld. Gollancz, 1936.

—— LIFAR (S.) : *Sergei Diaghilev ; his life, his work, his legend : an intimate biography.* Pl. 399 pp. Ld. Putnam, 1940.

FOKINE (M.) :

—— BEAUMONT (C. W.) : *Michael Fokine and his ballets.* 177 pp. Ld. Beaumont, 1935.

HASKELL (A. L.) : *Ballet, a complete guide to appreciation.* Ill. (Pelican special.) 172 pp. Harmondsworth, 1938. Repr. 1943.

—— *Diaghilev. See :* DIAGHILEV (S.).

—— *Tamara Karsavina. See :* KARSAVINA (T.).

HOPPÉ (E. O.) : *Studies from the Russian ballet.* Fine Art Society, n.d.

HYDEN (W.) : *Pavlova. See :* PAVLOVA (A.).

IVCHENKO (V. Y.) [V. Svetlov, pseud.] : *Anna Pavlova. See :* PAVLOVA (A.).

KAMENEFF (V.) : *Russian ballet through Russian eyes.* 42 pp. Ld. Russian Book Shop, 1936.

KARSAVINA (T.) : *Theatre street ; reminiscences.* With foreword by Sir J. M. Barrie. 341 pp. N.Y. and Ld. Heinemann, 1931.

—— HASKELL (A. L.) : *Tamara Karsavina.* (Artists of the dance, 4.) 2nd ed. 36 pp. Pl. Ld. British-Continental, 1931.

LEGAT (N. G.) : *Ballet russe : memoirs of N. Legat.* Transl. with a foreword by Sir P. Dukes. Dedicatory poem by J. Masefield. Pl. 67 pp. Ld. Methuen, 1939.

—— *Story of the Russian school.* Transl. by Sir P. Dukes. (Artists of the dance, 8.) Pl. 87 pp. Ld. British-Continental, 1932.

LIEVEN (Prince P. A.) : *The birth of the Ballets Russes.* Transl. by L. Zarine. Pl. 377 pp. Boston. Houghton, 1936.

LIFAR (S.) : *Ballet, traditional to modern.* Transl. by C. W. Beaumont. Pl. 302 pp. Ld. Putnam, 1938.

—— *Sergei Diaghilev. See :* DIAGHILEV (S.).

MASSINE (L.) :

—— ANTHONY (G.) : *Massine : camera studies.* With an appreciation by S. Sitwell. Pl. 33 pp. Ld. Routledge, 1939.

NIJINSKY (V.): *Diary*. Transl. and ed. by R. Nijinsky. Pl. 187 pp. N.Y. Simon & Schuster, 1936; Ld. Gollancz, 1937.
—— BEAUMONT (C. W.): *Vaslev Nijinsky*. (Essays on dancing and dancers, 2.) Ill. 28 pp. Ld. Beaumont, 1932.
—— BOURMAN (A.) and LYMAN (D.): *The tragedy of Nijinsky*. Ill. 291 pp. Hale, Wittlesley House, 1937.
—— NIJINSKY (R.): *Nijinsky*. Foreword by P. Claudel. Ill. 447 pp. N.Y. Simon & Schuster, 1934; Ld. Gollancz, 1936.
OLIVEROFF (A.): *Flight of the swan; a memory of Pavlova*. *See*: PAVLOVA (A.).
PAVLOVA (A.):
—— BEAUMONT (C. W.): *Anna Pavlova*. (Essays on dancing and dancers, 1.) Ill. 24 pp. Ld. Beaumont, 1932.
—— DANDRÉ (V. E.): *Anna Pavlova*. Ill. 409 pp. N.Y. Goldberger, 1933; Ld. Cassell, 1932.
—— HYDEN (W.): *Pavlova: the genius of dance*. Ill. 208 pp. Re-issue. Ld. Constable, 1934.
—— IVCHENKO (V. Y.) [pseud. V. Svetlov]: *Anna Pavlova; a choreographic portrait*. (Artists of the dance.) 40 pp. Ill. Ld. British-Continental, c. 1930.
—— OLIVEROFF (A.): *Flight of the swan: a memory of Pavlova, as told to J. Gill*. Ill. 258 pp. N.Y. Dutton, 1932.
PROPERT (W. A.): *The Russian ballet, 1921–1929*. With a preface by J. E. Blanche. Pl. 103 pp. Ld. Lane, 1931.
SCHWEZOFF (I.): *Russian somersault*. Autobiography. 414 pp. N.Y. Harper, 1936.
—— With title: *Borzoi*. Ill. 441 pp. Ld. Hodder, 1935.
STOKES (A.): *Russian ballets*. 213 pp. Ld. Faber, 1935.
TERRY (Dame E.): *Russian ballet*. Ill. Indianapolis. Bobbs, 1913.
VALOIS (N. de): *Invitation to the ballet*. Ill. 304 pp. Ld. Lane, 1937; Oxf., 1938.

FINE ARTS

APLETIN (M.) ed.: *Painting, sculpture and graphic art in the U.S.S.R.* VOKS ill. Almanac, 1934.
BUXTON (D. R.): *Russian medieval architecture, with an account of the Transcaucasian styles and their influence in the west.* Pl. 112 pp. Cambridge Univ. Pr., 1934.
CHEN (J.): *Soviet art and artists.* 106 pp. Ld. Pilot Pr., 1944.

CONWAY (Sir W. M.) : *Art treasures in Soviet Russia*. Ill. 284 pp. Ld. Arnold, 1925.

FARBMAN (M. S.) ed. : *Masterpieces of Russian painting, 11th to 18th century*. Text by A. I. Anisimov and others. Pl. 124 pp. Ld. Europa, 1930.

FREEMAN (J.) and others, ed. : *Voices of October ; art and literature in Soviet Russia*. 317 pp. Ld. Vanguard Pr., 1930.

GRINDEA (M.) : *Soviet literature, art, music*. (Today's booklets. Adam international anthology.) 48 pp. Ld. Practical Pr., 1942.

HOLME (C. G.) ed. : *Art in the U.S.S.R.* (Studio Special.) Ill. 138 pp. Ld. Studio, 1935.

KONDAKOV (N. P.) : *The Russian icon*. Transl. by E. H. Minns. Ill. 226 pp. Oxf. Clarendon Pr., 1927.

LONDON (K.) : *The seven Soviet arts*. Transl. by E. Bensinger. Ill. 382 pp. Ld. Faber, 1937 ; N.Y. Yale Univ. Pr., 1938.

LOUKOMSKY (G. K.) : *History of modern Russian painting, 1840–1940*. 184 pp. Ld. Hutchinson, 1945.

LUNACHARSKY (A. V.) : *Selected works of art from the Fine Art Museum of the U.S.S.R, with notes and introduction*. (Art ed. of the Association of Painters of the Revolution, 1.) Pl. N.Y. Amkniga, 1930.

MILIUKOV (P. N.) : *Outlines of Russian culture*, pt. 3 : *Architecture, painting and music*. Ed. by M. Karpovich. 159 pp. Philadelphia. Univ. of Pennsylvania, 1942.

NEWMARCH (R. H.) : *The Russian arts*. Ill. N.Y. Dutton, 1916.

Soviet Literature, Art, Music. See : GRINDEA (M.).

TALBOT RICE (D.) ed. : *Russian art*. Publication in connection with the Exhibition of Russian Art, Belgrave Square, 1935. Ill. 136 pp. Ld. Guerney & Jackson, 1935.

IV. RUSSIAN LITERATURE, IN ENGLISH TRANSLATIONS, FROM THE 19TH CENTURY TO THE PRESENT TIME

ANTHOLOGIES: GENERAL

BECHHOFER (C. E.) [afterwards Roberts] ed. and partly transl.: *A Russian anthology in English.* 288 pp. Ld. Kegan Paul, 1917.

COURNOS (J.) ed.: *A treasury of Russian life and humour.* 676 pp. N.Y. Coward McCann, 1943. [Contains: prose, poetry and plays.]

FREEMAN (J.) and others, ed.: *Voices of October; art and literature in Soviet Russia.* 317 pp. Ld. Vanguard Pr., 1930.

GANGULEE (N. N.) ed.: *The Russian horizon; an anthology.* Foreword by H. G. Wells. 278 pp. Ld. Allen & Unwin, 1943. [Contains: quotations from prose and poetry.]

GRINDEA (M.): *Soviet literature, art, music.* (Today's booklets. Adam international anthology.) 48 pp. Ld. Practical Pr., 1942.

GUERNEY (B. G.) ed.: *Treasury of Russian literature, being a comprehensive selection of many of the best things by numerous authors.* With a foreword and biographical and critical notes. 1,048 pp. N.Y. Vanguard, 1943.

KONOVALOV (S.). *See under:* COLLECTIONS OF SHORT STORIES.

REAVEY (G.) and SLONIM (M.) ed. and transl.: *Soviet literature: an anthology.* 430 pp. Ld. Wishart, 1933. [Contains: stories and extracts from novels and poetry. Stories and extracts from: Babel; Bely; Bezimensky; Fadeev; Fedin; Gabrilovich; Gladkov; V. Ivanov; Kataev; Kaverin; Leonov; Olesha; Pasternak; Pilnyak; Remizov; Seifullina; Semenov; Sholokhov; Tikhonov; Zamyatin; Zoshchenko. Poetry by: Akhmatova; Bely; Bezimensky; Blok; Esenin; Gumilev; Klebnikhov; Mayakovsky; Pasternak; Selvinsky; Tikhonov; Tsvetaevna; Ushakov; Voloshin. With short biographical sketches and various essays.]

SELVER (P.) : *Anthology of modern Slavonic literature in prose and verse.* 348 pp. Ld. Kegan Paul, 1919. [Contains: Russian prose: Chekhov; Merezhkovsky; Sergeev-Tsensky; Shevchenko; Sologub. Russian poetry: Balmont; Bryusov; Gorodetsky; Hippius; V. Ivanov; Merezhkovsky; Minsky; Shevchenko; Sologub.]

Soviet Literature, Art, Music. See : GRINDEA (M.).

SPECTOR (I.) : *Golden age of Russian literature.* [An anthology.] N.Y. Lymanhouse, 1939. 258 pp. Caldwell. Caxton Printers, 1943.

UNDERWOOD (E.) : *The Slav anthology : Russian, Polish, Bohemian, Servian, Croatian.* 346 pp. Portland, Maine. Mosher, 1931.

Voices of October. See : FREEMAN (J.) and others.

VOYNICH (E. L.) : *Humour of Russia.* Ld. Scott, 1911.

WIENER (L.) ed. : *Anthology of Russian literature, from the earliest period to the present time.* 2 vols. N.Y. and Ld. Putnam, 1902–3. (Contains: bibliography of translations.]

ANTHOLOGIES : POETRY

BIANCHI (M. G. D.) ed. and transl. : *Russian lyrics and Cossack songs, done into Engl. verse.* 139 pp. N.Y. 1910.

BOWRA (C. M.) ed. : *A book of Russian verse.* Transl. by various hands. 127 pp. Ld. Macmillan, 1943. [Contains: Akhmatova; Annenski; Balmont; Baratynsky; Blok; Bryusov; Esenin; Fet; Gumilev; V. Ivanov; Kazin; Khodasevich; Khomyakov; Koltsov; Lermontov; Mandelstam; Mayakovsky; Maykov; Nekrasov; Pasternak; Polonsky; Pushkin; Sologub; Solovev; Surikov; Tolstoy; Tyuchev.]

CORNFORD (F.) and SALAMAN (E. P.) : *Poems from the Russian.* 74 pp. Ld. Faber, 1943. [Contains: Akhmatova; Balmont; Blok; Fet; Koltsov; Krylov; Lermontov; Maykov; Nekrasov; Pushkin; Tolstoy; Tyuchev.]

COXWELL (C. F.) ed. and transl. : *Russian poems.* With an introduction by D. S. Mirsky. 309 pp. Ld. Daniel, 1929. [Contains: Akhmatova; Annenski; Apukhtin; Balmont; Baratynsky; Batyushkov; Bely; Blok; Bryusov; Bunin; Fet; Glinka; Gumilev; Z. Hippius; V. Ivanov; Khomyakov; Koltsov; Krylov; Kuzmin; Lermontov; Mayakovsky; Maykov; Merezhkovsky; Minsky; Nadson; Nekrasov;

Nikitin; Ogarev; Pasternak; Pavlova; Polonsky; Pushkin; Sologub; Solovev; A. K. Tolstoy; Turgenev; Tyuchev; Voloshin; Yazykov; Zhukovský.]

DEUTSCH (B.) and YARMOLINSKY (A.) ed. and transl.: *Modern Russian poetry*. 179 pp. Ld. Lane, 1921.

—— Same, enlarged; with title: *Russian poetry: an anthology*. 254 pp. N.Y., 1927; Ld. Lawrence, 1929. [Contains: Akhmatova; Balmont; Baratynsky; Bedny; Bely; Bezimensky; Blok; Bryusov; Bunin; Chulkov; Esenin; Ehrenburg; Fet; Gastev; Gerasimov; Gorodetsky; Z. Hippius; V. Ivanov; Kazin; Klyuev; Koltsov; Kuzmin; Lermontov; Mayakovsky; Maykov; Merezhkovsky; Minsky; Nekrasov; Oreshin; Polonsky; Pushkin; Severyanin; Sologub; Solovev; A. K. Tolstoy; Tyuchev; Voloshin.]

ELTON (O.): *Verse from Pushkin and others*. 188 pp. Ld. Arnold, 1935. [Contains: Akhmatova; Blok; Nekrasov; Pushkin; Tyuchev.]

JARINTZOV (N.): *Russian poets and poems*. Vol. 1: *Classics*. 357 pp. Oxf. Blackwell, 1917.

KAUN (A. S.): *Soviet poets and poetry*. 208 pp. Berkeley. Univ. of California Pr., 1943.

KRUP (J.): *Six poems from the Russian*. 317 pp. N.Y. Galleon Pr., 1936.

MATHESON (P. E.): *Holy Russia, and other poems*. 63 pp. Ld. Oxf. Univ. Pr., 1918. [Contains: Fet; Koltsov; Krasov; Lermontov; Nadson; Nekrasov; Nikitin; Ogarev; Pushkin; Shishkov; A. K. Tolstoy; Tyuchev; Yazykov; Zhukovsky.]

New Directions, anthology in prose and poetry. Ed. by J. Laughlin. 729 pp. Norfolk. New Directions, Connecticut, 1941. [Contains: pp. 513–650 a chapter: "Soviet Russian poetry; a survey, translations and critical essays." On poets: Bagritsky; Khodasevich; Kirsanov; Lugovskoy; Mayakovsky; Outkin; Pasternak; Selvinsky; Svetlov; Tikhonov; Zharov.]

POLLEN (J.): *Russian songs and lyrics*. 191 pp. Ld. East & West, 1916.

RUDZINSKY (B. A.) ed. and transl.: *Selections of Russian poetry*. 102 pp. Ld. Blackie, 1918.

SELVER (P.) ed. and transl.: *Modern Russian poetry*. Texts and transl. 65 pp. Ld. Kegan Paul, 1917. [Contains: Balmont; Blok; Bryusov; Bunin; Z. Hippius; Merezhkovsky; Minsky; Sologub; Solovev.]

SHELLEY (G.) ed. and transl.: *Modern poems from Russia*. 93 pp. Ld. Allen & Unwin, 1942. [Contains: Akhmatova;

Balmont; Bely; Blok; Ehrenburg; Esenin; Gumilev; Klyuev; Mayakovsky; Merezhkovsky; Pasternak; Sologub; Zharov.]

SOSYURA (V.): *Poems of Soviet Ukraine.* Transl. by M. Trommer. N.Y. Trommer, 1939.

TROMMER (M.): *Poems by women poets of Russia.*

COLLECTIONS OF SHORT STORIES

CHAMOT (A. E.) ed. and transl.: *Selected Russian short stories.* 344 pp. Ld. Oxf. Univ. Pr., 1925. (World's classics.) [Contains: Chekhov; Dostoevsky; Garshin; Gogol; Gorky; Kuprin; Lermontov; Pushkin; Turgenev.]

COURNOS (J.) ed. and transl.: *Short stories out of Soviet Russia.* 206 pp. Ld. Dent, 1929; reissued 1932. [Contains: Alekseev; Babel; V. Ivanov; Kataev; Leonov; Lidin; Pilnyak; Prishvin; Sergeev-Tsensky; A. N. Tolstoy; Zozulya.]

FEN (E.) ed. and transl.: *Modern Russian stories.* 244 pp. Ld. Methuen, 1943. [Contains: Babel; Fedin; Leonov; Neverov; Pilnyak; Romanov; A. N. Tolstoy; Zoshchenko.]

FEN (E.) ed. and transl.: *Soviet stories of the last decade.* 212 pp. Ld. Methuen, 1945. [Contains: Bramm and Grinberg; Dikovsky; Dolghih; Ehrenburg; Gorbatov; Kozhevnikov; Lidin; Malyshkin; Roonova; Shoshin; Simonov; Sokolov-Nikitov.]

FRIEDLAND (L. S.) and PIROSHNIKOFF (J. R.): *Flying Osip; stories of New Russia.* 318 pp. Ld. Unwin, 1925.

GRAHAM (S.): *Great Russian short stories.* 1,021 pp. Ld. Benn, 1929. [Contains: Afanasev; Alekseev; Andreev; Apukhtin; Babel; Bryusov; Bunin; Chekhov; Chirikov; Doroshovich; Dostoevsky; Ertel; Garshin; Gogol; Gorky; Kataev; Kuprin; Okulev; Pilnyak; Pushkin; Romanov; Sologub; Solovev; L. N. Tolstoy; Turgenev; Zhukovsky; Zoshchenko.]

KONOVALOV (S.) ed.: *Bonfire: stories out of Soviet Russia; an anthology of contemporary Russian literature.* 320 pp. Ld. Benn, 1932. [Contains: Babel; Chetverikov; Ehrenburg; Fadeev; Fedin; Fibikh; V. Ivanov; Kataev; Lebedinsky; Leonov; Lidin; Neverov; Ognev; Olesha; Pilnyak; Romanov; Semenov; Shklovsky; A. N. Tolstoy; Vesely; Yakovlev; Zamyatin; Zayaitsky; Zoshchenko.]

KOTELIANSKY (S. S.) ed. and partly transl. : *Russian short stories.*
156 pp. Ld. Allen Lane, Penguin Books, 1941. [Contains:
Bunin; Chekhov; Garshin; Kuprin,]

MONTAGU (I.) and MARSHALL (H.) ed. : *Soviet short stories*; 1st
series. (Life and literature in the Soviet Union, 2.) 154 pp.
Ld. Pilot Pr., 1942. [Contains: Ardov; Ehrenburg;
Isbach; Kerash; Lidin; Olesha; Pavstovsky; Platonov;
Tynyanov; Zoshchenko.]

MONTAGU (I.) and MARSHALL (H.) ed. : *Soviet short stories, 1942–
43*; 2nd series. (Life and literature in the Soviet Union, 5.)
121 pp. Ld. Pilot Pr., 1943. [Contains: Gorbatov;
Isbach; Kassil; Pavstovsky; Petrov; Shpanov; Sholokhov;
Simonov; Sobolev; Tikhonov; Wassilevska.]

MONTAGU (I.) and MARSHALL (H.) ed. : *Soviet short stories, 1944*;
3rd series. (Life and literature in the Soviet Union.) 152 pp.
Ld. Pilot Pr., 1944. [Contains: Dovzhenko; Gorbatov;
Ilenkov; Kaverin; Knorre; Kozhevnikov; Lavrenov;
Simonov; Tikhonov; Trenyev.]

ROBBINS (J. J.) and KUNITZ (J.) ed. and transl. : *Azure cities:
stories of New Russia.* (Modern books.) 320 pp. Ld.
Mod. Bks. Ltd., 1929. [Contains: Babel; Ivanov; Liashko;
Lidin; Neverov; Pilnyak; Romanov; Seifullina; Shaginian;
Shishkov; A. Tolstoy; Volkov; Zoshchenko.]

RODKER (J.) ed. : *Soviet anthology ; short stories by Soviet writers.*
231 pp. Ld. Cape, 1943. [Contains: Babel; Bergelson;
Freirman; Gorky; Grossman; Kataev; Kaverin; Lench;
Pavlenko; Pavstovsky; Pilnyak; Raskin; Slobodsky;
Tikhonov; Virta; Volosov; Weissenberg; Zoshchenko.]

Russian Short Stories. 448 pp. Ld. Faber, 1943. [Contains:
Andreev; Babel; Bunin; Chekhov; Dostoevsky; Garshin;
Gogol; Gorky; V. Ivanov; Kataev; Kuprin; Leonov;
Lermontov; Leskov; Prishvin; Pushkin; Sergeev-Tsensky;
Sologub; L. N. Tolstoy; Turgenev.]

SCHWEIKERT (H. C.) ed. : *Russian short stories.* Rev. ed. Ld.
Scott, 1919.

Soviet Short Stories. See : MONTAGU (I.) and MARSHALL (H.).

Soviet War Stories. 192 pp. Ld. Hutchinson, 1943; Heinemann, 1944. [Contains: Panferov; Gorbatov; Sholokhov;
K. Simonov; Wassilewska.]

TOWNSEND (R. S.) : *Short stories by Russian authors.* 275 pp.
(Everyman's Library.) Ld. Dent, 1924. [Contains:
Andreev; Chekhov; Chirikov; Gogol; Gorky; Korolenko;
Kuprin; Pushkin; Sologub; L. N. Tolstoy.] Repr. 1943.

YARMOLINSKY (A.) ed.: *A treasury of great Russian short stories.* 1,018 pp. N.Y. Macmillan, 1944.

COLLECTIONS OF PLAYS

BECHHOFER (C. E.) [afterwards Roberts] transl.: *Five Russian plays, with one from the Ukrainian.* 173 pp. Ld. Kegan Paul; N.Y. Dutton, 1916. [Contains: Chekhov; Evreinov; Fonvizin; Ukrainka.]

BLAKE (B.) ed.: *Four Soviet plays.* 427 pp. Ld. Lawrence & Wishart, 1937. [Contains: Gorky; Kocherga; Pogodin; Vishnevsky.]

Four Soviet War Plays. 208 pp. Ld. Hutchinson, 1943. [Contains: Korneichuk; Leonov; K. Simonov.]

LYONS (E.) ed.: *Six Soviet plays.* 608 pp. Ld. Gollancz, 1935. (Contains: Afinogenev; Bulgakov; Glebov; Kataev; Kirshon; Pogodin.]

NOYES (G. R.) ed. and partly transl.: *Masterpieces of the Russian drama.* With an introduction. 902 pp. Ld. and N.Y. Appleton, 1933. [Contains: Andreev; Chekhov; Fonvizin; Gogol; Gorky; Griboedov; Mayakovsky; Ostrovsky; Pisemsky; A. K. Tolstoy; L. N. Tolstoy; Turgenev.]

SAYLER (O. M.) ed.: *Moscow Art Theatre series of Russian plays.* First series. Transl. by J. Covan. N.Y. Brentano's, 1923. 5 vols. and 1 vol. ed. [Contains: Chekhov; Gorky; A. K. Tolstoy.]

—— Second series. N.Y. Brentano's, 1923. [Contains: Chekhov; Dostoevsky; Ostrovsky.]

FOLK-LITERATURE, INCLUDING PROVERBS

BAIN (R. N.) ed. and transl.: *Cossack fairy tales and folk tales.* 290 pp. Ld. Lawrence & Bullen (1st ed. 1894), new ed. 1902.

—— *Russian fairy tales.* Ld. Lawrence (1st ed. 1893), 3rd ed. 1915.

BAUER–CZARNOMSKI. (F.): *Proverbs in Russian and English.* 103 pp. Ld. 1920.

BLUMENTHAL (V. de) ed.: *Folk tales from the Russian.* 153 pp. Ld. 1903.

The Book of the Bear. Being twenty-one tales newly translated by J. E. Harrison and H. Mirrlees. Ld. Nonesuch Pr., 1926.

CHADWICK (H. M.) and CHADWICK (N. K.): *The growth of literature,* vol. 2: *Russian oral literature.* Ld. Cambridge Univ. Pr., 1936.

CHADWICK (N. K.): *Russian heroic poetry.* 294 pp. Ld. Cambridge Univ. Pr., 1932.

CHAMPION (S. G.) ed.: *Racial proverbs; a selection of the world's proverbs* [in English]. 767 pp. Ld. Routledge, 1938. [Contains, pp. 255–77, a list of 790 Russian and 202 Ukrainian proverbs. Introduction by A. I. Guershoon.]

COXWELL (C. F.) ed. and transl.: *Siberian and other folk tales; primitive literature of the empire of the Tsar.* With introduction and notes. 1,056 pp. Ld. Daniel, 1925.

DOLE (N. H.) ed. and transl.: *The Russian fairy book.* 126 pp. N.Y., 1907.

ENTWISTLE (W. J.): *European balladry.* Book 2, chapter 4: 'Russian ballads.' Oxf. Clarendon Pr., 1939.

GUERSHOON (A. I.): *Certain aspects of Russian proverbs.* 204 pp. Ld. Muller, 1941. [Contains: List of 1,361 Russian proverbs in English translation.]

HAPGOOD (I. F.): *Epic songs of Russia.* Ld. (1st ed. 1886), 2nd ed. 1915.

HOUGHTON (L. S.): *The Russian grandmother's wonder tales.* 348 pp. N.Y. Scribner, 1906.

KAUN (A. S.): *Folk trends in Soviet poetry.* (*In: New Directions in prose and poetry,* pp. 569–95. 1941.)

MAGNUS (L. A.): *The heroic ballads of Russia.* [A study with prose summaries.] 210 pp. Ld. Kegan Paul, Trench, Trubner, 1921.

—— *Russian folk tales.* 350 pp. Ld. Mitford, 1915.

The tale of the armament of Igor. See: The tale of the armament of Igor.

MICHELL (R.) and others: *The chronicle of Novgorod.* Ld. 1914.

PULMAN (S.) ed. and transl.: *Children's story from Russian fairy tales and legends.* 144 pp. Philadelphia. McKay, 1925.

SEGAL (L.): *Russian proverbs and their English equivalents.* N.Y. Dutton, 1917.

ZEITLIN (I.) ed.: Skazki: *Tales and legends of old Russia.* (Contains translations of some of Pushkin's folk tales in verse.] 335 pp. N.Y. 1926.

*The Tale of the Armament of Igor, a.d. 1185 ; a Russian historical
epic.* Ed. and transl. by L. A. Magnus. With rev. Russian
text. (Publications of the Philological Society.)   122 pp.
Ld. Oxf. Univ. Pr., 1915.

WORKS OF INDIVIDUAL AUTHORS

AFANASEV (Aleksandr), 1826–71.
> *Death and the soldier.* Transl. by R. Graham. (*In :* S. Graham,
> *Great Russian short stories*, 1929.)

AFINOGENEV (Aleksandr Nikolaevich), 1900–41.
> *Distant point* ; a play. Transl. and adapted by H. Griffith. Songs
> freely adapted by G. Parsons. 95 pp. Ld. Cape & Pushkin
> Pr., 1941.
> *Fear* ; a play in four acts and nine scenes. Authorised translation,
> by C. Malamuth. (*In :* E. Lyons, *Six Soviet plays*, 1935.)
> *Fear* ; transl. by N. Strelsky, D. B. Colman and A. Greene. N.Y.
> Poughkeepsie, 1934.
> *Listen, professor !* A play in three acts. Acting version by
> P. Phillips. 78 pp. Pl. N.Y. French, 1944.

AKHAMATOVA (Anna) [pseud. of Anna Andreevna Gorenko], 1888–.
> *All is plundered.* (*In :* Reavey and Slonim, *Soviet Literature*, 1933.)
> *Forty-seven love poems.* Transl. by N. Duddington. 64 pp. Ld.
> Cape, 1927.
> Poems. (*In :* C. M. Bowra, *A book of Russian verse*, 1943.)
> Poems. (*In :* F. Cornford and E. P. Salaman, *Poems from the
> Russian*, 1943.)
> Poems. (*In :* C. F. Coxwell, *Russian poems*, 1929.)
> Poems. (*In :* G. Shelley, *Modern poems from Russia*, 1942.)
> Poem. (*In :* O. Elton, *Verse from Pushkin and others*, 1935.)

AKSAKOV (Sergei Timofeevich), 1791–1859.
> *Chronicles of a Russian family.* Transl. by M. C. Beverley. N.Y.
> Dutton ; Ld. Routledge, 1924. (Broadway translations.)
> [Translation of the whole of *Family chronicle*, 3 chapters of
> *Years of childhood*, of *Bagrov, the grandson*, and the first 3
> parts of *Recollections*.]
> *Notes on angling.* (*In :* A. Ransome, *Rod and line*. Ld. Cape,
> 1932. Pp. 244–86.
> *Years of childhood.* Transl. by J. D. Duff. 340 pp. Ld.
> Arnold, 1916.

—— Same. 446 pp. Ld. Oxf. Univ. Pr., 1923. (World's classics.) [Contains also: *The scarlet flower*, a short story.]

A Russian gentleman, Transl. by J. D. Duff. 209 pp. Ld. Arnold, 1917.

—— Same. 283 pp. Ld. Oxf. Univ. Pr., 1923. (World's classics.) [Transl. of *Family chronicle*.]

A Russian schoolboy. Transl. by J. D. Duff. 216 pp. Ld. Arnold, 1917.

—— Same. 288 pp. Ld. Oxf. Univ. Pr., 1924. (World's classics.) [Contains: transl. of *Recollections*, and *Butterfly collecting*.]

Biography, criticism, etc. :

OSBOURNE (E. A.) comp. : *Early translations from the Russian* : 5. S. T. Aksakov. (Bookman. Ld. 1932.)

ALDANOV (Mark) [pseud. of Mark Aleksandrovich Landau], 1888–.

The devil's bridge. Transl. by A. E. Chamot. 325 pp. N.Y. and Ld. Knopf, 1928. [Second part of the trilogy, *The ninth thermidor*.]

The fifth seal. Transl. by N. Wreden. 482 pp. N.Y. Scribner, 1943.

The key. Transl. by E. Gellibrand. 327 pp. Ld. Harrap, 1931.

The ninth thermidor. Transl. by A. E. Chamot. 377 pp. N.Y. Knopf, 1926. (First part of the trilogy.]

Saint Helena : little island. Transl. by A. E. Chamot. 193 pp. Ld. Jarrolds, 1924. [Third part of the trilogy, *The ninth thermidor*.]

ALEICHEM (Shalom) [pseud. of Shalom Rabinowitz], 1859–1916.

Jewish children. Transl. from the Yiddish by H. Berman. 268 pp. Ld. Heinemann, 1920; N.Y. Knopf, 1926.

Stempenyu. Transl. by H. Berman. Ld. Methuen, 1913.

Biography, criticism, etc. :

SAMUEL (M.)

The world of Sholom Aleichem. N.Y. Knopf, 1943.

ALEKSANDER (Irina) [pseud., of Irina Kunina.]

Running tide. Transl. by B. G. Guerney. 264 pp. N.Y. Duell, 1943.

ALEKSEEV (Gleb), 1892–.

Diphtheria. Transl. by L. Zarine. (*In :* S. Graham, *Great Russian short stories*, 1929.)

Other eyes. (*In :* J. Cournos, *Short stories out of Soviet Russia*, 1932.)

ANDREEV (Leonid Nikolaevich), 1871–1919.
> Plays: *The black maskers*; *The life of man*; *The Sabine women.*
> Transl. by C. L. Meader and F. N. Scott. With an introduction
> by V. V. Brusyanin. Ld. Duckworth; N.Y. Scribner, 1915.

Abyss. Transl. by J. Cournos. 31 pp. Waltham St. Lawrence.
Golden Cockerell Pr., 1929.

Anathema; a tragedy in seven scenes. Transl. by H. Bernstein.
N.Y. Macmillan, 1910.

And it came to pass that the king was dead. Transl. by M.
Magnus. 46 pp. Ld. Daniel, 1921.

—— Same, with title: *When the king loses his head, and other
stories.* Transl. by A. J. Wolfe. N.Y. International Book
Publishing Co., 1920. (Russian authors' library.)

The confessions of a little man during the great days. Transl. by
R. S. Townsend. 242 pp. Ld. Duckworth, 1917. [Russian
title: *The yoke of war.*]

The crushed flower, and other stories. 361 pp. Ld. Duckworth,
1917.

The dark. Transl. by L. A. Magnus and K. Walter. 52 pp.
Richmond. L. & V. Woolf, 1922.

The dear departing; a frivolous performance in one act. Transl.
by J. West. 32 pp. Ld. Hendersons, 1916.

A dilemma. Transl. by J. Cournos. Philadelphia. Brown, 1910.

—— Same, with title: *Dilemma; a story of mental perplexity.*
Transl. by J. Cournos. 114 pp. N.Y. Greenberg, n.d.

He who gets slapped: a play in four acts. Transl. with an introduction by G. Zilboorg. N.Y. and Ld. Brentano's, 1922.

He who gets slapped; a novel adapted by G. A. Carlin from L.
Andreev's drama, and the Victor Seastoom photo-play. Ill.
with scenes from the photo-play. 273 pp. N.Y. Grosset.
1925.

His excellency the governor. Transl. by M. Magnus. 96 pp. Ld.
Daniel, 1921.

*Judas Iscariot, forming with Eleazor and Ben Tobit a biblical
trilogy.* Transl. by W. H. Lowe. 192 pp. Ld. Griffiths,
1910.

Katerina (*Yekaterina Ivanovna*); a drama in four acts. Authorised
transl. from the original MS. with a preface by H. Bernstein.
N.Y. and Ld. Brentano's, 1923 and 1924.

Life of man; a play in five acts. Transl. by C. J. Hogarth. 141 pp.
N.Y. Macmillan; Ld. Allen & Unwin, 1915.

The little angel, and other stories. 255 pp. Ld. Hodder &
Stoughton, 1915. (Great Russian Fiction.)

—— Same. Transl. by W. H. Lowe. N.Y. Knopf, 1916. (Borzoi Pocket Books.)

The little angel. Repr. from the ed. published by Hodder & Stoughton, 1915. (*In:* S. Graham, *Great Russian short stories,* 1929.)

Love one's neighbour. Transl. by T. Seltzer. Boni, 1914; N.Y. Shay, 1917.

The red laugh. Fragments of a discovered manuscript. Transl. by A. Linden. 117 pp. Ld. Fisher Unwin, 1905; N.Y. Duffield, 1915.

Roerich; a monograph of a great artist. N.Y. Brentano's, 1925.

Samson in chains. [Posthumous tragedy.] Authorised transl. from the original MS. by H. Bernstein. N.Y. Brentano's, 1923.

Sashka Jigouleff. Transl. by L. Hicks. 287 pp. Ld. Jarrolds, 1926.

—— Same, with introduction by M. Gorky. 294 pp. N.Y. MacBride, 1925. (Russian Masterpieces, 2.)

Satan's diary. Transl. by H. Bernstein. N.Y. Boni & Liveright, 1920.

Savva; The life of man. Two plays. Transl. with an introduction by T. Seltzer. N.Y. Little, 1914. (Modern Drama Series.)

The seven who were hanged. Authorised transl. by H. Bernstein. N.Y. Ogilvie, 1909.

—— Same. 80 pp. Ld. Fifield, 1909.

—— Same. Transl. by H. Bernstein. 190 pp. Cleveland World publ., 1941.

Silence. Transl. by J. Cournos. Philadelphia. Brown, 1908. Also published by Frank Maurice, N.Y.

Silence, and other stories. Transl. by W. H. Lowe. 219 pp. Ld. Griffiths, 1910.

The sorrows of Belgium: a play in six scenes. Authorised transl. by H. Bernstein. 132 pp. N.Y. Macmillan, 1915.

To the stars; a drama. Transl. by M. Magnus. 84 pp. Ld. 1921. (Plays for a People's Theatre, 10.)

The waltz of the dogs; a play in four acts. Authorised transl. from the original MS. by H. Bernstein. 141 pp. Ld. Brentano's, 1924. (Printed in U.S.A.)

Biography, criticism, etc.:

GORKY (M.): *Reminiscences of Leonid Andreev.* Transl. by K. Mansfield and S. S. Koteliansky. 128 pp. Ld. Heinemann, 1931; Ld. Dulau, 1928; N.Y. Random House, 1928.

GORKY (M.): *Reminiscences of Tolstoy, Chekhov and Andreev.*
Ld. Hogarth Pr., 1934.
KAUN (A. S.): *Leonid Andreev; a critical study.* 361 pp. N.Y.
Huebsch. Viking Pr., 1924.
ANNENSKI (Innokenti Fedorovich), 1856–1909.
Poems. (*In:* C. M. Bowra, *A book of Russian verse,* 1943.)
Poems. (*In:* C. F. Coxwell, *Russian poems,* 1929.)
APUKHTIN (Aleksei Nikolaevich), 1841–93.
The Archive of Countess D . . . (*In:* S. Graham, *Great Russian short stories,* 1929.)
From death to life. Transl. by R. Frank and E. Huybers. N.Y.
Frank, 1917. (Gems of Russian Literature.)
Poems. (*In:* C. F. Coxwell, *Russian poems,* 1929.)
ARDOV (Victor).
Happy ending. (*In:* I. Montagu and H. Marshall, *Soviet short stories,* 1942.)
ARSENIEV (Vladimir Klavidevich), 1872–.
Dersu, the Trapper; a hunter's life in Ussuria. Transl. by M.
Burr. Ill. 352 pp. Ld. Secker & Warburg, 1939; N.Y.
Dutton, 1941.
ARTEM VESELY. *See:* VESELY (Artem).
ARTSYBASHEV (Boris Mikhailovich), 1899–.
Poor Shaydullah. Told and ill. by the author. Ld. Macmillan,
1931.
Seven Simeons; a Russian tale. Retold and ill. by the author.
Ld. Cassell, 1937.
ARTSYBASHEV (Mikhail Petrovich), 1878–1927.
Breaking point. Ld. Secker, 1915.
Jealousy. N.Y. Boni & Liveright, 1923.
The millionaire; Ivan Lande; Nina. Three novelettes. Transl. by
P. Pinkerton. Ld. Secker, 1915.
Sanine. Transl. by P. Pinkerton. Ld. Secker, 1915. New ed.
327 pp. N.Y. Viking Pr., 1926.
—— Same. Preface by E. Boyd. 380 pp. N.Y. 1931.
(Modern Library of the World's Best Books.)
The savage. Transl. by G. Cannan and A. Strindberg. N.Y. Boni
& Liveright, 1924.
Tales of the Revolution. Transl. by P. Pinkerton. Ld. Secker,
1917.
War; a play in four acts. Transl. by T. Seltzer. N.Y. Knopf
1916.
War. Transl. by P. Pinkerton and I. Ozhol. Ld. Richards,
1918.

ASH (Shalom), 1880–.

Three novels: Uncle Moses; Chaim Lederer's return; Judge not.
3 vols. (in 1). Transl. by E. Krauch. 176, 116, 127 pp. N.Y.
Putnam, 1938.

Apostle. Transl. by M. Samuel. 804 pp. N.Y. Putnam, 1943.

Children of Abraham; short stories. Transl. by M. Samuel.
433 pp. N.Y. Putnam, 1942.

The mother. Transl. by N. Ausuebel. 357 pp. N.Y. Liveright,
1930.

—— Same. Authorised transl. by E. Krauch. 295 pp. N.Y.
Grosset, 1940. (Novels of Distinction.)

Mottke, the thief. Transl. by W. and E. Muir. 314 pp. N.Y.
Putnam, 1935.

Nazarene. Transl. by M. Samuel. 698 pp. N.Y. Putnam,
1939.

Sabbatai Zevi; a tragedy in three acts and six scenes, with a
prologue and an epilogue. Authorised transl. by F. Whyte and
G. R. Noyes. 131 pp. Ill. N.Y. Jewish publ., 1930.

Salvation. Transl. by W. and E. Muir. 332 pp. N.Y. Putnam,
1934.

Song of the valley. Transl. by E. Krauch. 245 pp. N.Y. Putnam,
1939; Ld. Routledge.

Three cities; a trilogy. Transl. by W. and E. Muir. Special ed.
899 pp. N.Y. Putnam, 1943.

The war goes on. Transl. by W. and E. Muir. 528 pp. N.Y.
Putnam, 1936.

—— Same, with title: *Calf of paper.* Cheap ed. Ld.
Gollancz, 1938.

What I believe. Transl. by M. Samuel. 201 pp. N.Y. Putnam,
1941.

—— Same, with title: *My personal faith.* 201 pp. Ld.
Routledge, 1942.

AVDEENKO (Aleksandr Evstigneevich).

I love : a novel. Transl. by A. Wixley. 283 pp. Ld. Lawrence,
1935.

BABEL (Isaak Emmanuilovich), 1894–.

The awakening. (*In:* G. Reavey and M. Slonim, *Soviet literature,*
1933.)

Benia Krik: a film novel. Transl. by I. Montagu and S. S.
Nolbandov. 96 pp. Ltd. ed. Ld. Collet, 1935.

The birth of a king. (*In:* E. Fen, *Modern Russian stories,* 1943.)

The death of Dolgushov. (*In:* J. Cournos, *Short stories out of
Soviet Russia,* 1929.)

—— Same. (*In*: S. Konovalov, *Bonfire*, 1932.)

End of St. Ipaty. (*In*: G. Reavey and M. Slonim, *Soviet literature*, 1933.)

Gedali. (*In*: S. Konovalov, *Bonfire*, 1932.)

Karl-Yankel. Transl. by A. Brown. (*In*: J. Rodker, *Soviet anthology*, 1943.)

The letter. (*In*: J. Cournos, *Short stories out of Soviet Russia*, 1929.)

—— Same. Transl. by A. Brown. (*In*: J. Rodker, *Soviet anthology*, 1943.)

Life and adventures of Matvey Pavlichenko. Transl. by J. Harland. (*In*: S. Graham, *Great Russian short stories*, 1929.)

Red cavalry. Transl. by J. Harland. Ld. Knopf, 1929.

Salt. (*In*: J. Cournos, *Short stories out of Soviet Russia*, 1929.)

BAGRITSKY (Edouard), 1895–1934.

Poems. (*In*: *New Directions in prose and poetry*, 1941.)

BALMONT (Konstantin Dmitrievich), 1867–.

Poems. (*In*: C. M. Bowra, *A book of Russian verse*, 1943.)

Poems. (*In*: F. Cornford and E. P. Salaman, *Poems from the Russian*, 1943.)

Poems. (*In*: C. F. Coxwell, *Russian poems*, 1929.)

Poems. (*In*: B. Deutsch and A. Yarmolinsky, *Russian poetry*, 1929.)

Poems. (*In*: P. Selver, *Modern Russian poetry*, 1917, and his: *Anthology of modern Slavonic literature*, 1919.)

BARATYNSKY (Evgeny Abramovich), 1800–44.

Poems. (*In*: C. M. Bowra, *A book of Russian verse*, 1943.)

Poems. (*In*: C. F. Coxwell, *Russian poems*, 1929.)

Poems. (*In*: B. Deutsch and A. Yarmolinsky, *Russian poetry*, 1929.)

BASHKIRTSEVA (Maria Konstantinova), 1860–84.

Journal of a young artist. New ed. N.Y. Dutton, 1926.

Biography, criticism, etc.:

CAHUET (A.): *Moussia; the life and death of Maria Bashkirtseva.* Transl. by K. Wallis. Ill. 300 pp. N.Y. Macaulay, 1929.

BATYUSHKOV (Konstantin Nikolaevich), 1787–1855.

Dying Tasso. (*Extract in*: L. Wiener, *Russian anthology*, vol. 2, 1903.)

BEDNY (Demyan) [pseud. of Efim Alekseevich Pridvorov], 1883–.

Poems. (*In*: B. Deutsch and A. Yarmolinsky, *Russian poetry*, 1929.)

BELINSKY (Visarion Grigorevich), 1811–48.

The natural school. (*In*: L. Wiener, *Russian anthology*, 1903.)

BELY (Andrey) [pseud. of Boris Nikolaevich Bugaev], 1880–1934.
  Kotik Letaev. (*Extract in:* G. Reavey and M. Slonim, *Soviet literature*, 1933.)
  Poem: *Christ is risen.* (*Extract in:* B. Deutsch and A. Yarmolinsky, *Russian poetry*, 1929.)
  Russia. (*In:* G. Reavey and M. Slonim, *Soviet literature*, 1933.)
BERGELSON (David).
  The Russian for parallel. Transl. by S. Garry. (*In:* J. Rodker, *Soviet anthology, short stories*, 1943.)
BEZIMENSKY (Aleksandr Ilyich), 1882–.
  Poems. (*In:* G. Reavey and M. Slonim, *Soviet literature*, 1933.)
  Poem: *Village and factory,* (*In:* B. Deutsch and A. Yarmolinsky, *Russian poetry*, 1929.)
BILL–BELOTSERKOVSKY (Vladimir Naumovich), 1884–.
  Life is calling: a play in four acts. Transl. by A. Wixley. 88 pp. Ld. Lawrence & Wishart, 1938; N.Y. International Publishers, 1938.
BLOK (Aleksandr Aleksandrovich), 1880–1921.
  The collapse of humanism. Transl. by I. Berlin. (*In: The Oxford Outlook*, Oxf. Blackwell, 1931.)
  New America. (*In:* G. Reavey and M. Slonim, *Soviet literature*, 1933.)
  Poems. (*In:* C. M. Bowra, *A book of Russian verse*, 1943.)
  Poems. (*In:* F. Cornford and E. P. Salaman, *Poems from the Russian*, 1943.)
  Poems. (*In:* B. Deutsch and A. Yarmolinsky, *Russian poetry*, 1929.)
  Poems. (*In:* O. Elton, *Verse from Pushkin and others*, 1935.)
  The twelve. Transl. by C. E. Bechhofer. Ld. Chatto & Windus, 1920.
  —— Same. Transl. by B. Deutsch and A. Yarmolinsky. N.Y. Rudge, 1931.
  —— Same. (*Extract in:* G. Reavey and M. Slonim, *Soviet literature*, 1933.)
  Biography, criticism, etc.:
  BOWRA (C. M.): *Alexander Blok.* (*In his: The heritage of symbolism*, 1943.)
  LAVRIN (J.): *Alexander Blok.* (*In his: Aspects of modernism*, 1936.)
BRAMM (M.) and GRINBERG (I.).
  The friends. (*In:* E. Fen, *Soviet stories of the last decade*, 1945.)
BRYUSOV (Valery Yakovlevich), 1873–1924.
  Fiery angel: a sixteenth century romance. Transl. by I. Montagu and S. Nolbandov. 392 pp. Ld. Cayme Pr., 1930.

The marble bust. (*In :* S. Graham, *Great Russian short stories,* 1929.)

Poems. (*In :* C. M. Bowra, *A book of Russian verse,* 1943.)

Poems. (*In :* C. F. Coxwell, *Russian poems,* 1929.)

Poems. (*In :* P. Selver, *Modern Russian poetry,* 1917. *And in his : Anthology of modern Slavonic literature,* 1919.)

The republic of the southern cross, and other stories. Transl. by R. Graham. Ld. Constable, 1918. (Constable's Russian library.) [Contains : 'The republic of the southern cross'; 'Rhea Silvia'; 'The marble bust'.]

Rhea Silvia. (*In :* S. Graham, *Great Russian short stories,* 1929.)

BUGAEV (Boris Nikolaevich), *see :* BELY (Andrey) [pseud. of Boris Nikolaevich Bugaev.]

BULGAKOV (Mikhail Afanasevich), 1891–.

Days of the turbines ; a play. [Based on the novel, *The white guard.*] Authorised transl. by E. Lyons. (*In :* E. Lyons, *Six Soviet plays,* 1935.)

BUNIN (Ivan Alekseevich), 1870–.

The dreams of Chang, and other stories. Transl. by B. G. Guerney. N.Y. Knopf, 1923.

—— Same. With title on cover : *Fifteen tales.* Ld. Secker, 1924.

Early passions. Ld. Pallas, 1939.

The Elaghin affair, and other stories. Selected and transl. by B. G. Guerney. 297 pp. N.Y. Knopf, 1935.

The gentleman from San Francisco, and other stories. Transl. by D. H. Lawrence, S. S. Koteliansky and L. Woolf. 86 pp. Richmond. L. & V. Woolf, 1922. 2nd ed. Ld. Hogarth Pr., 1934.

—— Same. Authorised transl. by B. G. Guerney. 313 pp. N.Y. Knopf, 1933. Repr. 1941. (Albla Books.)

Grammar of love. Transl. by J. Cournos. 221 pp. Ld. L. & V. Woolf, 1935. (U.S.A. printed.)

Mitya's love. Transl. from the French by M. Boyd. With an introduction by E. Boyd. 212 pp. N.Y. Holt, 1926.

Never-ending spring. Transl. by H. C. Matheson. (*In :* S. Graham, *Great Russian short stories,* 1929.)

Poems. (*In :* C. F. Coxwell, *Russian poems,* 1929.)

Poems. (*In :* P. Selver, *Modern Russian poetry,* 1917.)

Sunstroke. Transl. by H. C. Matheson. (*In :* S. Graham, *Great Russian short stories,* 1929.)

The village. Transl. by I. F. Hapgood. 291 pp. Ld. Secker, 1923 ; N.Y. Knopf, 1933.

The well of days. Transl. by G. Struve and H. Miles. 351 pp. Ld. Hogarth Pr., 1933; N.Y. Knopf, 1934.
CHEKHOV (Anton Pavlovich), 1860–1904.
The tales of Tchehov. Transl. by C. Garnett. 13 vols. Ld. Chatto & Windus; N.Y. Macmillan, 1916–1922:
Vol. 1. *The darling, and other stories.* Introduction by E. Garnett. [Contains: 'The darling'; 'Tolstoy's criticism on the darling'; 'Ariadne'; 'Polinka'; 'Anyuta'; 'The two Volodyas'; 'The trousseau'; 'The helpmate'; 'Talent'; 'An artist's story'; 'Three years'.]
Vol. 2. *The duel, etc.* [Contains: 'The duel'; 'Excellent people'; 'Mire'; 'Neighbours'; 'At home'; 'Expensive lessons'; 'The princess'; 'The chemist's wife'.]
Vol. 3. *The lady with the dog, etc.* [Contains: 'The lady with the dog'; 'A doctor's visit'; 'An upheaval'; 'Ionitch'; 'The head of the family'; 'The black monk'; 'Volodya'; 'An anonymous story'; 'The husband'.]
Vol. 4. *The party, etc.* [Contains: 'The party'; 'Terror'; 'A woman's kingdom'; 'A problem'; 'The kiss'; 'Anna on the neck'; 'The teacher of literature'; 'Not wanted'; 'Typhus'; 'A misfortune'; 'A trifle from life'.]
Vol. 5. *The wife, etc.* [Contains: 'The wife'; 'Difficult people'; 'The grasshopper'; 'A dreary story'; 'The privy councillor'; 'The man in a case'; 'Gooseberries'; 'About love'; 'The lottery ticket'.]
Vol. 6. *The witch, etc.* [Contains: 'The witch'; 'Peasant wives'; 'The post'; 'The new villa'; 'Dreams'; 'The pipe'; 'Agafya'; 'At Christmas time'; 'Gusev'; 'The student'; 'In the ravine'; 'The huntsman'; 'Happiness'; 'A malefactor'; 'Peasants'.]
Vol. 7. *The bishop, etc.* [Contains: 'The bishop'; 'The letter'; 'Easter eve'; 'A nightmare'; 'The murder'; 'Uprooted'; 'The Steppe'.]
Vol. 8. *The chorus girl, etc.* [Contains: 'The chorus girl'; 'Verotchka'; 'My life'; 'At a country house'; 'A father'; 'On the road'; 'Rothschild's fiddle'; 'Ivan Matveyitch'; 'Zinotchka'; 'Bad weather'; 'A gentleman friend'; 'A trivial incident'.]
Vol. 9. *The schoolmistress, etc.* [Contains: 'The schoolmistress'; 'A nervous breakdown'; 'Misery'; 'Champagne'; 'After the theatre'; 'A lady's story'; 'In exile'; 'The cattle dealers'; 'Sorrow'; 'On official duty'; 'The first-class passenger'; 'A tragic actor'; 'A transgression'; 'Small

fry'; 'The requiem'; 'In the coach house'; 'Panic fears';
'The bet'; 'The head-gardener's story'; 'The beauties';
'The shoemaker and the devil'.]

Vol. 10. *The horse-stealers, etc.* [Contains: 'The horse-stealers';
'Ward No. 6'; 'The Petchenyeg'; 'A dead body'; 'A
happy ending'; 'The looking-glass'; 'Old age'; 'Darkness'; 'The beggar'; 'A story without a title'; 'In trouble';
'Frost'; 'A slander'; 'Minds ferment'; 'Gone astray';
'An avenger'; 'The jeune premier'; 'A defenceless
creature'; 'An enigmatic nature'; 'A happy man'; 'A
troublesome visitor'; 'An actor's end'.]

Vol. 11. *The schoolmaster, etc.* [Contains: 'The schoolmaster';
'Enemies'; 'The examining magistrate'; 'Betrothed';
'From the diary of a violent tempered man'; 'In the
dark'; 'A play'; 'A mystery'; 'Strong impressions';
'Drunk'; 'The Marshall's widow'; 'A bad business';
'In the court'; 'Boots'; 'Joy'; 'Ladies'; 'A peculiar man';
'At the barber's'; 'An inadvertence'; 'The album'; 'Oh!
the public'; 'A tripping tongue'; 'Overdoing it'; 'The
orator'; 'Malingerers'; 'In the graveyard'; 'Hush!'; 'In
an hotel'; 'In a strange land'.]

Vol. 12. *The cook's wedding, etc.* [Contains: 'The cook's wedding'; 'Sleepy'; 'Children'; 'The runaway'; 'Grisha';
'Oysters'; 'Home'; 'A classical student'; 'Vanka'; 'An
incident'; 'A day in the country'; 'Boys'; 'Shrove
Tuesday'; 'The old house'; 'In Passion week'; 'White
brow'; 'Kashtanka'; 'A chameleon'; 'The dependents';
'Who was to blame?'; 'The bird market'; 'An adventure'; 'The fish'; 'Art'; 'The Swedish match'.]

Vol. 13. *Love, etc.* [Contains: 'Love'; 'Lights'; 'A story without
an end'; 'Mari d'Elle'; 'A living chattel'; 'The doctor';
'Too early'; 'The cossack'; 'Aborigines'; 'An enquiry';
'Martyrs'; 'The lion and the sun'; A daughter of Albion';
'Choristers'; 'Nerves'; 'A work of art'; 'A joke'; 'A
country cottage'; 'A blunder'; 'Fat and thin'; 'The
death of a government clerk'; 'A pink stocking'; 'At a
summer villa'.]

Select tales of Tchehov. Transl. by C. Garnett. 849 pp. Ld.
Chatto & Windus, 1927. [Contains: 'The lady with the dog';
'The horse-stealers'; 'The bishop'; 'In the ravine'; 'Sleepy';
'Ionitch'; 'At Christmas time'; 'My life'; 'The chorus girl';
'The new villa'; 'The teacher of literature'; 'The witch'; 'An
anonymous story'; 'The beauties'; 'A transgression';

'Gusev'; 'A woman's kingdom'; 'Mire'; 'Easter eve'; 'A dreary story'; 'A misfortune'; 'Happiness'; 'The darling'.]

Tales from Tchehov. Transl. by C. Garnett. 248 pp. Ld. Penguin Books, 1938.

The plays of Tchehov. Transl. by C. Garnett. 2 vols. Ld. Chatto & Windus; N.Y. Macmillan, 1923–24.

Vol. 1. 'The cherry orchard'; 'Uncle Vanya'; 'The seagull'; 'The bear'; 'The proposal'.

Vol. 2. 'Three sisters'; 'Ivanov'; 'A swansong'; 'An unwilling martyr'; 'The anniversary'; 'On the high road'; 'The wedding'.

Plays and stories. Transl. by S. S. Koteliansky. 360 pp. Ld. Dent, 1937. (Everyman's Library.)

Five famous plays by Anton Chekhov: 'The bear', 'The three sisters', 'The cherry orchard', transl. by J. West; 'Uncle Vanya', 'The seagull', transl. by M. Fell. 311 pp. Ld. Duckworth, 1939.

Plays. Transl. by M. Fell. N.Y., 1912. [Contains: 'Uncle Vanya'; 'Ivanov'; 'The seagull'; 'The swansong'.]

Two plays. Transl. by G. Calderon. N.Y. and Ld., 1912. [Contains: 'The seagull'; 'The cherry orchard'.]

A bear. Transl. by R. T. A. House. N.Y. Moods, 1919,

The bet, and other stories. Transl. by S. S. Koteliansky and J. M. Murry. Boston. Luce, 1915.

The cherry orchard. (*In:* O. M. Sayler, *Moscow Art Theatre series of Russian plays,* series 1, 1923.)

The black monk, and other stories. Transl. by R. E. C. Long. Ld. Duckworth, 1903; N.Y. Stokes, 1915.

In a foreign land. (*In:* P. Selver, *Anthology of modern Slavonic literature,* 1919.)

Ivanov. (*In:* O. M. Sayler, *Moscow Art Theatre series of Russian plays,* series 2, 1923.)

The jubilee. (*In:* C. E. Bechhofer, *Five Russian plays,* 1916.)

The kiss, and other stories. Transl. by R. E. C. Long. Ld. Duckworth, 1908; N.Y. Scribner, 1912.

My life. Transl. by E. R. Schimanskaya. 106 pp. Ld. King & Staples, 1943. (Modern Readers' Library.)

The pass, and other stories. Transl. by R. E. C. Long. 317 pp. N.Y. Scribner, 1912.

Russian silhouettes; more Russian stories. Transl. by M. Fell. 318 pp. N.Y. Scribner, 1915.

The shooting party. Transl. by A. E. Chamot. 244 pp. Ld. Stanley Paul, 1926.

The Steppe, and other stories. Transl. by A. Kaye. 296 pp. N.Y. Stokes, 1915.

Stories of Russian life. Transl. by M. Fell. 314 pp. N.Y. Scribner, 1914.

That worthless fellow Platonov. Transl. by J. Cournos. 279 pp. Ld. Dent, 1930.

The three sisters. (*In:* O. M. Sayler, *Moscow Art Theatre series of Russian plays,* series 1, 1923.)

—— Same. Transl. by S. Young. N.Y. French, 1941.

Uncle Vanya. (*In:* O. M. Sayler, *Moscow Art Theatre series of Russian plays,* series 1, 1923.)

—— Same. Transl. by R. Caylor. N.Y. Covici, 1930.

The wedding. (*In:* C. E. Bechhofer, *Five Russian plays,* 1916.)

The wood demon. Transl. by S. S. Koteliansky. 120 pp. Ld. Chatto & Windus, 1926. [The first version of Uncle Vanya.]

Letters of Anton Tchehov to his family and friends. Transl. by C. Garnett, with a biographical sketch. Ld. Chatto & Windus; N.Y. Macmillan, 1920.

Letters to Olga Leonardovna Knipper. Transl. by C. Garnett. 387 pp. N.Y. Doran; Ld. Chatto & Windus, 1926.

Letters on the short story, the drama and other literary topics. Selected and ed. by L. S. Friedland. 346 pp. Ld. Bles, 1924.

Life and letters of Anton Tchehov. Transl. and ed. by S. S. Koteliansky and P. Tomlinson. 315 pp. Ld. Cassell, 1925.

Literary and theatrical reminiscences. Transl. and ed. by S. S. Koteliansky. 248 pp. Ld. Routledge; N.Y. Doran, 1927. [Unpublished work of Chekhov, with miscellaneous essays and reminiscences by various authors.]

The note books of Anton Tchekhov, together with Reminiscences of Tchekhov, by Gorky. Transl. by S. S. Koteliansky and L. Woolf. Ld. Hogarth Pr.; N.Y. Huebsch, 1921.

Biography, criticism, etc.:

HEIFETZ: *Bibliography of Chekhov's works translated into English and published in America. Bulletin of Bibliography,* May 13, N.Y., 1929.

BARING (M.): *Plays of Anton Tchekhov.* (*In his: Landmarks of Russian literature.* Ld., 1916.)

ELTON (O.): *Chekhov.* Oxf. Clarendon Pr., 1929. (Taylorian Lecture, 1929.) Repr. in his: *Essays and addresses.* Ld. Arnold, 1939.

GERHARDI (W.): *Anton Chekhov; a critical study.* Ld. Cobden-Sanderson, 1923.

MURRY (J. M.) : *Aspects of literature.* 203 pp. N.Y. Knopf, 1920. [Contains essay on Chekhov.]

MURRY (J. M.) : *Discoveries : essays in literary criticism.* 313 pp. Ld. Collins, 1924. [Contains essay on Chekhov.]

SHESTOV (L.) : *Anton Chekhov, and other essays.* Transl. by S. S. Koteliansky and J. M. Murry. Ld. 1916.

TOUMANOVA (N. A.) : *Anton Chekhov, the voice of twilight Russia.* 239 pp. Ld. Cape, 1937.

CHETVERIKOV (D.).

> *Corpses.* (*In :* S. Konovalov, *Bonfire,* 1932.)

CHIRIKOV (Evgeny Nikolaevich), 1864–.

> *Bound over.* Transl. by L. Zarine. (*In :* S. Graham, *Great Russian short stories,* 1929.)
>
> *The magician.* Transl. by L. Zarine (ibid.).
>
> *Marka of the pits.* Transl. by L. Zarine. 223 pp. N.Y. Alston Rivers, 1930.

CHULKOV (Georgiy), 1879–.

> Poems. (*In :* B. Deutsch and A. Yarmolinsky, *Modern Russian poetry,* 1923.)

CHUVOVSKY (Korney Ivanovich), 1883–.

> *Crocodile.* With the original Russian illustrations. Transl. by B. Deutsch. 31 pp. N.Y. Lippincott, 1931 ; Ld. Mathews, 1932.

DANILEVSKY (Grigoriy Petrovich), 1829–90.

> *Moscow in flames.* Transl. by A. S. Rappoport. Ld. Stanley Paul, 1917.

DIKOVSKY (Sergey).

> *The commandant of the isle of birds.* (*In :* E. Fen, *Soviet stories of the last decade,* 1945.)

DOLGHIH (A.).

> *Raw stuff.* (*In :* E. Fen, *Soviet stories of the last decade,* 1945.)

DOROSHEVICH (Vasiliy), 1864–.

> *How Hassan lost his trousers.* Transl. by R. Graham. (*In :* S. Graham, *Great Russian short stories,* 1929.)

DOSTOEVSKAYA (Anna Grigorevna), 1846–1918.

> *The diary of Dostoevsky's wife.* Ed. by R. Fülöp-Miller and F. Eckstein. Transl. from the German by M. Pemberton. 421 pp. Ld. Gollancz, 1928.
>
> *Dostoevsky portrayed by his wife : the diary and reminiscences of Mme Dostoevsky.* Transl. and ed. by S. S. Koteliansky. Ld. Routledge, 1926.

DOSTOEVSKAYA (Lyubov Fedorovna), 1869–.

> *The emigrant.* Transl. by V. Margolies. With an introduction by S. Graham. Ld. Constable, 1916.

DOSTOEVSKY (Fedor Mikhailovich), 1821–81.
> *The novels of Fyodor Dostoevsky.* From the Russian by Constance
> Garnett. Ld. Heinemann, 1912–1920. 12 vols.
> Vol. 1. *The Brothers Karamazov.* 1912.
> Vol. 2. *The idiot.* 1913.
> Vol. 3. *The possessed.* 1913.
> Vol. 4. *Crime and punishment.* 1914.
> Vol. 5. *The house of the dead.* 1915.
> Vol. 6. *The insulted and injured.* 1915.
> Vol. 7. *A raw youth.* 1916.
> Vol. 8. 'The eternal husband'; 'The double'; 'A gentle spirit'.
> 1917.
> Vol. 9. 'The gambler'; 'Poor people'; 'The landlady'. 1917.
> Vol. 10. 'White nights'; 'Notes from underground'; 'A faint
> heart'; 'A Christmas tree and a wedding'; 'Polzunkov';
> 'A little hero'; 'Mr. Prohartchin'. 1918.
> Vol. 11. 'An honest thief'; 'Uncle's dream'; 'A novel in nine
> letters'; 'An unpleasant predicament'; 'Another man's
> wife'; 'The heavenly Christmas tree'; 'The peasant
> Marey'; 'The crocodile'; 'Bobuk'; 'The dream of a
> ridiculous man'. 1919.
> Vol. 12. 'A friend of the family'; 'Nyetochka Nyezhanov'. 1920.
> *The Brothers Karamazov.* Transl. by C. Garnett. 2 vols. Ld.
> Dent 1927. (Everyman's Library.)
> —— Same. (*In :* O. M. Sayler, *Moscow Art Theatre of Russian
> plays*, series 2, 1923.)
> *Buried alive. See : The house of the dead.* 1911.
> *Crime and punishment : a Russian realistic novel.* 455 pp. Ld.
> Dent, 1915. (Everyman's Library.) (Repr. of 1911.)
> *Crime and punishment.* Transl. by C. Garnett. Ill. 531 pp.
> N.Y. A. S. Barnes, 1944. (Illustrated Modern Library.)
> *The gambler. See : Poor folk,* and *The gambler.* 1915.
> *The grand inquisitor.* [Parts 2–3, Book 5, Chapter 4 of *The Brothers
> Karamazov.*] Transl. by S. S. Koteliansky. With an intro-
> duction by D. H. Lawrence. 81 pp. Ld. Secker,
> 1935.
> *The house of the dead; or, Prison life in Siberia.* Ld. Dent, 1911.
> (Everyman's Library.) Repr. of *Buried alive,* ed. of 1881 and
> 1887.
> *The idiot.* Transl. by E. M. Martin. 605 pp. Ld. Dent, 1914.
> (Everyman's Library.)
> —— Same. Transl. by C. Garnett. 586 pp. N.Y. Modern
> Library, 1942. (Modern Library Giants.)

Letters from the underworld, and other tales. Transl. by C. J. Hogarth. Ld. Dent, 1913. (Everyman's Library.) [Contains: 'Letters from the underworld'; 'The gentle maiden'; 'The landlady'.]

A nasty story. Transl. by A. E. Chamot. (*In:* A. E. Chamot, *Selected Russian short stories*, 1925.)

—— Same. With title: *An unpleasant predicament. See: The novels of F. Dostoevsky.* Transl. by C. Garnett, vol. 11, 1919.

Poor folk, and *The gambler.* Transl. by C. J. Hogarth. Ld. Dent, 1915. (Everyman's Library.)

The possessed. 2 vols. Ld. Dent, 1931. (Everyman's Library.) Repr. of *The novels of F. Dostoevsky.* Transl. by C. Garnett, vol. 3, 1913.

Stavrogin's confession. Transl. by S. S. Koteliansky and V. Woolf. Ld. Hogarth Pr., 1922. [Contains: three unpublished chapters from *The possessed,* and the plan of *The life of a great sinner,* of which *The Brothers Karamazov* was intended to be part.]

Pages from the journal of an author. Transl. by S. S. Koteliansky and J. Middleton Murry. London and Dublin. Maunsell, 1916. (The Modern Russian Library.) Boston. Luce, 1916. [Contains: 'The dream of a queer fellow', and 'Pushkin'.]

Letters of F. M. Dostoevsky to his family and friends. Transl. from the German by Ethel C. Mayne. Ld. Chatto & Windus, 1914. [Contains: 77 letters of Dostoevsky, recollections of Dostoevsky by Grigorevich, etc., contemporary judgments of Aksakov, Turgenev, Tolstoy, etc., and a chronological table of Dostoevsky's life.]

Letters of Dostoevsky to his wife. Translated by Elizabeth Hill and Doris Mudie. Ld. Constable, 1930.

Dostoevsky: letters and reminiscences. Translated by S. S. Koteliansky and J. M. Murry. Ld. Chatto & Windus; N.Y. Knopf, 1923. 286 pp. [Contains: letters from D. to his wife and friends and reminiscences by his wife.]

New Dostoevsky letters. Translated by S. S. Koteliansky. Ld. Mandrake Pr., 1929.

Biography, criticism, etc.:

OSBOURNE (E. A.): *Russian literature and translations,* 7: *F. M. Dostoevsky.* Bookman. Ld. June, 1933.

ABRAHAM (G.): *Dostoevsky.* Ld. Duckworth, 1936. (Great Lives.)

BERDYAEV (N. A.): *Dostoevsky: an interpretation.* Transl. by D. Attwater. Ld. Sheed, 1936; N.Y. 1934.

CARR (E. H.): *Dostoevsky; a new biography.* Ld. Allen & Unwin, 1931.

DOSTOEVSKAYA (A. G.): *Dostoevsky portrayed by his wife.* See: DOSTOEVSKAYA (A. G.).

DOSTOEVSKAYA (A. G.): *The diary of Dostoevsky's wife.* See: DOSTOEVSKAYA (A. G.).

DOSTOEVSKAYA (L. F.): *Fyodor Dostoevsky; a study.* 294 pp. Yale. Univ. Pr., 1922.

GIDE (A.): *Dostoevsky.* Transl. from the French, with an introduction, by Arnold Bennett. 224 pp. Ld. Dent; N.Y. Knopf, 1926.

LAVRIN (J.): *Dostoevsky and his creation: a psychocritical study.* 189 pp. Ld. Collins, 1920.

LAVRIN (J.): *Dostoevsky: a study.* Ld. Methuen, 1943. [New ed.]

LLOYD (J. A. T.): *A great Russian realist: Fedor Dostoieffsky.* Ld. Stanley Paul, 1912.

MEIER-GRAEFFE (J.): *Dostoevsky, the man and his work.* Transl. by H. H. Marks. 406 pp. Ill. N.Y. Harcourt, 1928.

MEREZHKOVSKY (D. S.): *Tolstoy as man and artist, with an essay on Dostoevsky.* Ld. Constable, 1902.

MUCHNIC (H.): *Dostoevsky's English reputation, 1881–1936.* 219 pp. Northampton, Mass. 1939. (Smith College Studies in Modern Languages, 20.) [Contains: Bibliography of books and articles in English on Dostoevsky.]

MURRY (J. M.): *Fyodor Dostoevsky: a critical study,* 264 pp. Boston. Small, 1924.

SIMMONS (E. J.): *Dostoevski: the making of a novelist.* Cambridge, Mass. Harvard Univ. Pr.; Ld. Oxf. Univ. Pr., 1940.

SOLOVYOV (E. A.): *Dostoevsky; his life and literary activity.* Transl. by C. J. Hogarth. Ld. Allen & Unwin, 1916.

YARMOLINSKY (A.): *Dostoevsky: a life.* 447 pp. N.Y. Harcourt, 1931.

YARMOLINSKY (A.): *Dostoevsky: a study in his ideology.* N.Y., 1921.

ZERNOV (N.): *Three Russian prophets: Khomyakov, Dostoevsky, Soloviev.* 171 pp. Ld. Student, 1944.

ZWEIG (St.): *Three masters: Balzac, Dickens, Dostoevsky.* Transl. from the German by E. and C. Paul. 238 pp. N.Y. Viking Pr.; Ld. Allen & Unwin, 1930.

DOVZHENKO (Aleksandr).
  Mother Stoyan. (*In:* I. Montagu and H. Marshall, *Soviet short stories*, 1944.)
  The night before the battle. (Ibid.)
DYMOV (Osip) [pseud. of O. I. Perelman], 1878–.
  The flight from the cross. Transl. by G. M. Foakes. Ld. Werner Laurie, 1916.
  Nju; an everyday tragedy. Transl. by R. Ivan. N.Y. 1917. (Borzoi Books.)
EHRENBURG (Ilya Grigorevich), 1891–.
  The call. (*In:* E. Fen, *Soviet stories of the last decade*, 1945.)
  Extraordinary adventures of Julio Jurenito and his disciples. Transl. by U. Vanzler. 399 pp. N.Y. Covici, 1930.
  The fall of Paris. Transl. by G. Shelley. 382 pp. Ld. Hutchinson, 1942.
  —— With title: *The fall of Paris, seen through Soviet eyes.* Foreword by S. T. Warner. Ld. Modern Books, 1941.
  The love of Jeanne Ney. Transl. by H. C. Matheson. 356 pp. Ld. Davies, 1929.
  New short stories. (*In:* I. Montagu and H. Marshall, *Soviet short stories.* Ld. 1942.)
  Out of chaos. Transl. by A. Bakshy. 391 pp. N.Y. Holt, 1934. [Russian title: *The second day.*]
  Protochny lane. (*In:* S. Konovalov, *Bonfire*, 1932.)
  A Soviet writer looks at Vienna. Transl. by I. Montagu. 47 pp. Ld. Lawrence, 1934.
  A street in Moscow. Transl. by S. Volochova. 278 pp. Ld. Grayson, 1933.
ERSHOV (Petr Pavlovich), 1815–69.
  Humpy. Transl. by W. C. White. 110 pp. N.Y. Harper, 1931.
  Little hunchback horse. Adaptation from a poem [by Ershov] by I. Wicker. 155 pp. N.Y. Putnam, 1942.
  Little magic horse, a Russian tale. Transl. by T. B. Drowne. Ill. Macmillan, 1942.
ERTEL (Aleksandr Ivanovich), 1855–1908.
  A greedy peasant, and *A specialist.* Transl. by N. Duddington. (*In:* S. Graham, *Great Russian short stories*, 1929.)
ESENIN (Sergey), 1895–1925.
  Poems. (*In:* C. M. Bowra, *A book of Russian verse*, 1943.)
  Poems. (*In:* B. Deutsch and A. Yarmolinsky, *Russian poetry*, 1929.)

The tramp; The last village poet; My mysterious world; Tavern Moscow. (*In*: G. Reavey and M. Slonim, *Soviet literature*, 1933.)

EVREYNOV (Nikolai Nikolaevich), 1879–.

Chief things: a comedy for some, a drama for others. Theatre Guild acting version made from the translation by H. Bernstein and L. Randoll. 226 pp. N.Y. Doubleday, 1926.

The beautiful despot. (*In*: C. E. Bechhofer, *Five Russian plays* 1916.)

The corridors of the soul, a monodrama. Adapted by P. Wilde from the Vienna version of F. T. Csokor. (*In*: P. Wilde, *Contemporary one-act plays from nine countries.* Ld. Harrap, 1936.)

The merry death. (*In*: C. E. Bechhofer, *Five Russian plays*, 1916.)

Theatre in life. Ed. and transl. by A. I. Nazaroff. With an introduction by O. M. Sayler. 296 pp. Ld. Harrap; N.Y. Brentano's, 1927.

The theatre of the soul. Transl. by M. Potapenko and C. St. John. Ld. Hendersons, 1915.

FADEEV (Aleksandr Aleksandrovich), 1901–.

Annihilation. (*In*: S. Konovalov, *Bonfire*, 1932.)

The bandits, from *The last of the Udegs.* (*In*: G. Reavey and M. Slonim, *Soviet literature*, 1933.)

The nineteen. Transl. by R. D. Charques. 293 pp. Ld. Lawrence, 1929. [Russian title: *The rout.*]

FEDIN (Konstantin Aleksandrovich), 1892–.

The chronicle of Narovchat. (*In*: E. Fen, *Modern Russian stories*, 1943.)

Love and war, from *The brothers.* (*In*: G. Reavey and M. Slonim, *Soviet literature*, 1933.)

The orchard. (*In*: S. Konovalov, *Bonfire*, 1932.)

FET (Afanasy Afanasevich), afterwards Shenshin, 1820–92.

Poem: *Nocturne.* (*In*: P. E. Matheson, *Holy Russia*, 1918.)

Poems. (*In*: C. M. Bowra, *A book of Russian verse*, 1943.)

Poems. (*In*: F. Cornford and E. P. Salaman, *Poems from the Russian*, 1943.)

Poems. (*In*: B. Deutsch and A. Yarmolinsky, *Russian poetry*, 1929.)

FIALKO (Nathan Moisevich), 1881–.

The new city. Transl. from the Russian and rev. by the author. 153 pp. N.Y. Margent Pr., 1937.

FIBIKH (Daniel).

The execution. (*In*: S. Konovalov, *Bonfire*, 1932.)

FIGNER (Vera Nikolaevna), 1852–.

Memoirs of a revolutionist. Authorised transl. by C. C. Daniels and G. A. Davidson. Ed. by A. Kaun. 318 pp. N.Y. International Publ. Co., 1927.

FRANKO (Ivan Yakovlevich), 1856–1916.

Moses; a poem. Transl. from the Ukrainian by W. Semenyna, with a biographical sketch by S. Shumeyko. 93 pp. N.Y. United Ukrainian Organisation of the U.S., 1938.

Voice from Ukrainia. Biographical sketch and transl. from his works by P. Cundy. 74 pp. Manitoba. Buffy, 1932.

FREIRMAN (R.).

Pathless. Transl. by A. Brown. (*Extract in:* J. Rodker, *Soviet anthology*, 1943.)

FURMANOV (Dmitri Andreevich), 1891–1926.

Chapayev. 483 pp. N.Y. International Publishers, 1935.

—— Same. Cheap ed. 336 pp. Ld. Lawrence, 1936.

—— Same. (Workers' Library.) 311 pp. Ld. Lawrence, 1941.

GABRILOVICH (Evgeny).

The year 1930. (*In:* G. Reavey and M. Slonim, *Soviet literature,* 1933.)

GARSHIN (Vsevelod Mikhailovich), 1855–88.

The crimson flower. Transl. by R. Graham. (*In:* S. Graham, *Great Russian short stories,* 1929.)

Four days. Transl. by H. C. Matheson. (*In:* S. Graham, *Great Russian short stories,* 1929.)

—— Same. Transl. by S. S. Koteliansky. (*In: Russian short stories,* 1943.)

The red flower. Anon. transl. 37 pp. Philadelphia. Brown, 1911.

The signal, and other stories. Transl. by R. Smith. Ld. Duckworth; N.Y. Knopf, 1915. [Contains: 'Four days'; 'Nadjeda Nikolaevna'; 'The signal'.]

GASTEV (Aleksey Kapitonovich), 1882–.

Poems. (*In:* B. Deutsch and A. Yarmolinsky, *Russian poetry,* 1929.)

GERASIMOV (Mikhail Prokofevich), 1889–.

Poem. (*In:* B. Deutsch and A. Yarmolinsky, *Russian poetry,* 1929.)

Poems. (*In:* G. Z. Patrick, *Popular poetry in Soviet Russia,* 1929.)

GERMAN (Yuri Pavlovich), 1910–.

Alexei the gangster. Transl. by S. Garry. 288 pp. Ld. Routledge, 1940.

Antonina. Transl. by S. Garry. 470 pp. Ld. Routledge, 1937.

—— Same. With title: *Tonia.* 412 pp. N.Y. Knopf, 1938.

GLADKOV (Fedor Vasilevich), 1883–.
>   *Cement.* Transl. by A. S. Arthur and C. Ashleigh. 311 pp. Ld.
>   Lawrence, 1929.
>   *The ragged brigade*, from *Power.* (*In:* G. Reavey and M.
>   Slonim, *Soviet literature*, 1933.)

GLEBOV (Anatoliy Glebovich), 1899–.
>   *Inga; a play in four acts and thirteen scenes.* Transl. by C.
>   Malamuth. (*In:* E. Lyons, *Six Soviet plays*, 1935.)

GLINKA (Fedor Nikolaevich), 1788–1880.
>   *Poems.* (*In:* C. F. Coxwell, *Russian poems*, 1929.)

GOGOL (Nikolay Vasilevich), 1809–52.
>   *The works of Nikolay Gogol.* From the Russian by C. Garnett.
>   6 vols. Ld. Chatto & Windus, 1922–1928.
>   Vols. 1–2. *Dead souls.*
>   Vol. 3. *The overcoat, and other stories.* [Contains: 'The over-
>   coat'; 'The carriage'; 'The Nevsky prospect'; 'A
>   madman's diary'; 'The prisoner'; 'The nose'; 'The
>   portrait'.]
>   Vol. 4. *Evenings on a farm near Dinkanka.*
>   Vol. 5. *The government inspector, and other plays.* [Contains:
>   'The government inspector'; 'Marriage'; 'The
>   gamblers'; 'Dramatic sketches and fragments'.]
>   Vol. 6. 'Mirogod'; 'Old-world landowners'; 'Taras Bulba';
>   'Viy'; 'Tale of two Ivans'.
>   *Dead souls.* Transl. by C. J. Hogarth. 324 pp. Ld. Dent,
>   1915. (Everyman's Library.)
>   —— Same. Transl. by I. F. Hapgood. Reissued. Ld. Benn,
>   1929. (Essex Library.)
>   —— Same. With title: *Tchitchikoff's journeys.* Transl. by I. F.
>   Hapgood. Ld. Fisher Unwin, 1915. Repr. of ed. of 1886
>   and 1887.
>   *Diary of a madman.* Transl. by Prince D. S. Mirsky. Ill. 81 pp.
>   Ld. Cresset Pr., 1929. Ltd. ed.
>   *Evenings in Little Russia.* Transl. by E. W. Underwood and W. H.
>   Cline. 153 pp. Evanston. Lord, 1903. [Contains: 'The fair
>   of Sorotchinet'; 'An evening in May'; 'Midsummer evening'.]
>   *The gamblers.* Transl. by A. Berkman. N.Y. Macaulay, 1927.
>   *The inspector.* Transl. by J. L. Seymour and G. R. Noyes. (*In:*
>   G. R. Noyes, *Masterpieces of the Russian drama*, 1933.)
>   *The mantle, and other stories.* Transl. by C. Field. Ld. Laurie,
>   1915. [Contains: 'The mantle'; 'The nose'; 'A may-night'.]
>   *Marriage.* (*In:* E. L. Voynich, *Humour of Russia*, 1909.)
>   —— Same. Transl. by A. Berkman. N.Y. Macaulay, 1927.

Taras Bulba. Transl. by B. C. Badkerville. 295 pp. Ld. Scott, 1907.

Taras Bulba, and other tales. With an introduction by J. Cournos. Ld. Dent, 1918. (Everyman's Library.) Repr. 1930. [Contains: 'Taras Bulba'; 'St. John's eve'; 'Old-fashioned farmers'; 'How Ivan Ivanovitch quarrelled'; 'The portrait'; 'The cloak'; 'The king of the gnomes'; 'The calash'.]

Biography, criticism, etc.:

OSBOURNE (E. A.): Early transl. from the Russian: 4. *N. V. Gogol.* (*Bookman.* Ld. Oct. 1932.)

BARING (M.): *Gogol and the cheerfulness of the Russian people.* (*In his: Landmarks in Russian literature,* 1910.)

LAVRIN (J.): *Gogol.* 264 pp. Ld. Routledge, 1925; N.Y. Dutton, 1926. [Contains a bibliography.]

NABOKOV (V. V.): *Nikolay Gogol.* Connecticut. New Directions, 1942.

GOMBERG (Vladimir Germanovich). *See:* LIDIN (Vladimir) [pseud. of Vladimir Germanovich Gomberg.]

GONCHAROV (Ivan Aleksandrovich), 1812–91.

Oblomov. Transl. by C. J. Hogarth. 317 pp. [Abridged.] Ld. Allen & Unwin; N.Y. Macmillan, 1915.

—— Same. Transl. by N. Duddington. Ld. Allen & Unwin, 1929.

—— Re-issued. 517 pp. Ld. Dent, 1932. (Everyman's Libary.)

The precipice. Anon. transl. 319 pp. Ld. Hodder & Stoughton; N.Y. Knopf, 1915.

Biography, criticism, etc.:

DOBROLYUBOV (N. A.): *What is Oblomovism?* (*In:* L. Wiener, *Russian anthology,* vol. 2, 1903.)

GORBATOV (Boris).

After death. (*In:* I. Montagu and H. Marshall, *Soviet short stories,* 1944.)

Alexei Kulikov—Red armyman. (*In: Soviet war stories,* 1943.)

The trial of a comrade. (*In:* E. Fen, *Soviet stories of the last decade,* 1945.)

Zero hour. (*In:* I. Montagu and H. Marshall, *Soviet short stories,* 1943.)

GORENKO (Anna Andreevna). *See:* AKHMATOVA (Anna), pseud. of Anna Andreevna Gorenko.

GORKY (Maksim) [pseud. of Aleksey Maksimovich Peshkov], 1869–1936.

A book of short stories. Ed. by A. Yarmolinsky and M. Budberg. Foreword by A. Huxley. 403 pp. Ld. Cape, 1939.

A boy. Transl. by M. Budberg. (*In :* J. Rodker, *Soviet anthology,* 1943.)

Bystander. Transl. by B. G. Guerney. 729 pp. Ld. Cape, 1930. [The first pt. of the tetralogy, *The life of Klim Samghin.*]

Chelkash, and other stories. Transl. by E. Jakowleff and D. B. Montefiore. N.Y. Knopf, 1902.

—— Same. With title : *Twenty-six men and a girl.* Ld. Duckworth, 1902.

A confession. Transl. from the German by W. F. Harvey. Ld. Everett, 1910.

—— Same. Transl. by R. Strunsky. Ld. Stokes, 1916.

Creatures that once were men. Transl. by D. B. Montefiore and E. Jakowleff. (*In :* S. Graham, *Great Russian short stories,* 1929.)

—— Same. Transl. by J. K. M. Shirazi. With an introduction by G. K. Chesterton. Ld. Rivers; N.Y. Boni & Liveright, 1905.

Culture and the people. 224 pp. Ld. Lawrence & Wishart, 1939.

Days with Lenin. 64 pp. Ld. Lawrence, 1932.

Decadence. Transl. by V. Scott-Gatty. 324 pp. Ld. Cassell; N.Y. McBride, 1927.

Foma Gordyeeff. Transl. by I. F. Hapgood. Ld. Fisher Unwin; N.Y. Scribner, 1901.

—— Same. Transl. by H. Bernstein. N.Y. Ogilvie, 1901.

—— Same. With title : *Foma.* N.Y. Dimondstein, c. 1943.

—— Same. With title : *The man who was afraid.* Ld. Fisher Unwin, 1905. Repr. Ld. Benn, 1929.

Fragments from my diary. 320 pp. Ld. Allen, 1924.

—— Same. Repr. Ld. 1940 and 1942. (Penguin Books.)

—— Same. Transl. by M. Budberg. N.Y. McBride, 1924.

Heartache, and *The old woman Izerofel.* Transl. by A. S. Rappoport. Ld. Maclaren, 1905.

The individualists; Cain and Arteme; Strange companion. Transl. by A. S. Rappoport. Ld. Maclaren, 1906.

In the world. Transl. by G. M. Foakes. 464 pp. Ld. Laurie, 1917.

The judge. Transl. by M. Zakrevsky and B. H. Clark. N.Y. McBride, 1924.

Last plays. Transl. and adapted by Gibson-Cowan. 74 pp. N.Y. International Publishers, 1937; Ld. Lawrence & Wishart. [Contains : 'Yegot Bulichoff'; 'Dostigaeff and the others'.]

The life of Klim Samghin; or, *Forty years, the life of Klim Samghin.* A tetralogy. *See:* the separate pts., *Bystander*; *Magnet*; *Other fires*; *Specter.*

The lower depths. Transl. by L. Irving. Ld. Fisher Unwin, 1910.
—— Same. Transl. by J. Coran. (*In:* O. M. Sayler, *Moscow Art Theatre series of Russian plays,* 1st series, 1923.)
—— Same. With title: *Submerged.* Transl. by E. Hopkins. Boston. Four Seasons, 1915.
—— Same. With title: *At the bottom.* A new transl. by W. L. Laurence. 133 pp. N.Y. French, 1930.
—— Same. With title: *Down and out.* Transl. by G. R. Noyes and A. Kaun. (*In:* G. R. Noyeś, *Masterpieces of the Russian drama,* 1933.)

Magnet. Transl. by A. Bakshy. Ld. Cape, 1931. [The second pt. of the tetralogy, *The life of Klim Samghin.*]

The mother. N.Y. Appleton, 1907; Ld. Hodder & Stoughton, 1907. Repr. 1921.

My childhood. Transl. by G. M. Foakes. 308 pp. Ld. Laurie, 1915.

A naughty girl. Transl. by A. S. Rappoport. Ld. Maclaren, 1905.

On guard for the Soviet Union. Introduction by R. Rolland. 173 pp. Ld. Lawrence, 1933.

Orloff and his wife. Transl. by I. F. Hapgood. N.Y. Scribner, 1902.

Orloff and his wife : tales of the barefoot brigade. Transl. by I. F. Hapgood. N.Y. Scribner, 1901. [Contains: 'Orloff and his wife'; 'Konovaloff'; 'The khan and his son'; 'The exorcism'; 'Men with pasts'; 'The insolent man'; 'Varenka Olesoff'; 'Comrades'.]

The Orloff couple. Transl. by E. Yakovlev and D. B. Montefiore. Ld. Heinemann, 1901.

Other fires. Transl. by A. Bakshy. 507 pp. N.Y. Appleton, 1933. [The third pt. of the tetralogy, *The life of Klim Samghin.*]

The outcasts, and other stories. Ld. Fisher Unwin, 1902. [Contains: 'The outcasts'; 'Waiting for the ferry', both transl. by D. B. Montefiore. 'The affair of the clasps', transl. by V. Volkhovsky.] 2nd ed. 1910.

Reminiscences of Leonid Andreev. Transl. by K. Mansfield and S. S. Koteliansky. 118 pp. N.Y. Random House; Ld. Dulau, 1928; Ld. Heinemann, 1931.

Reminiscences of my youth. Transl. by V. Dewey. 344 pp. Ld. Heinemann, 1924,

—— Same. With title: *My university days.* 327 pp. N.Y. Boni & Liveright, 1924.

Reminiscences of Tolstoy. Transl. by S. S. Koteliansky and L. Woolf. 71 pp. Ld. Hogarth Pr., 1920; 115 pp. Hogarth Pr., 1921.

Reminiscences of Tolstoy, Chekhov and Andreev. Transl. by K. Mansfield, S. S. Koteliansky and L. Woolf. 191 pp. Ld. Hogarth Pr., 1934.

The specter. Transl. by A. Bakshy. 680 pp. N.Y. and Ld. Appleton, 1938. [The fourth pt. of the tetralogy, *The life of Klim Samghin.*]

The spy : The story of a superfluous man. Transl. by T. Seltzer. Ld. Duckworth; N.Y. Huebsch, 1908.

Stories of the Steppe. Transl. by H. T. Schnittkind and I. Goldberg. Boston. Stratford Co., 1918. [Contains: 'Makar Chudra' ; 'Because of monotony'.]

The story of a novel, and other stories. Transl. by M. Zahrkrevsky. 273 pp. N.Y. Dial Pr. ; Ld. Jarrolds, 1925. [Contains : 'The story of a novel' ; 'The sky blue life' ; 'An incident' ; 'The rehearsal' ; 'The hermit'.]

Tales. N.Y. Brentano's, 1923. [Contains : 'Twenty-six and one' ; 'Tchelkach' ; 'Malva'.]

Tales from Gorky. Transl. by R. N. Bain. Ld. Jarrolds; N.Y. Brentano's, 1902. [Contains : 'Chelkash' ; 'A rolling stone' ; 'In steppe' ; 'One autumn night' ; 'The green kitten' ; 'Comrades' ; 'Her lover' ; 'Chums' ; 'Twenty-six of us'.] Another issue by Funk & Wagnalls, 1902.]

—— Same. With title: *Chelkash, and other stories.* Transl. by R. N. Bain. Ld. Knopf, 1917.

Tales of two countries. [America and Italy]. Ld. Laurie; N.Y. Huebsch, 1914.

Three men. Transl. by C. Horne. Ld. Isbister, 1902.

—— Same. With title: *Three of them.* Transl. by A. Linden. Ld. Fisher Unwin, 1902; N.Y. Knopf, 1922.

Through Russia: a book of stories. Transl. by C. J. Hogarth. [Contains : 'Gubin' ; 'A woman' ; 'Kalinin' ; 'The birth of a man' ; 'The ice-breaker' ; 'Nilushka' ; 'The cemetery' ; 'On a river steamer' ; 'In a mountain defile' ; 'The dead man'.]

To American intellectuals. 31 pp. U.S.A. 1932. (International pamphlets, 28.)

Twenty-six and one, and other stories. Transl. by I. Stranik. N.Y. Taylor, 1902. [Contains : 'Twenty-six and one' ; 'Tchelkash' ; 'Malva'.]

Twenty-six men and a girl. Transl. by E. Yakovlev and D. B. Montefiore. Ld. Duckworth, 1902. [Contains: 'Twenty-six men and a girl'; 'Chelkash'; 'On a raft'; 'My fellow-travellers'.]

—— Same. Ed. by A. Yarmolinsky and M. Budberg. N.Y. Holt, 1939.

Yegor Bulichov and others: a play in three acts. Transl. by A. Wixley. (*In*: B. Blake, *Four Soviet plays*, 1937.)

Biography, criticism, etc. :

DILLON (E. J.) : *Maxim Gorky : his life and writings.* 390 pp. Ld. Isbister, 1902.

KAUN (A. S.) : *Maxim Gorky and his Russia.* 620 pp. Ld. Cape, 1932. [Contains a bibliography.]

OLGIN (M. J.) : *Maxim Gorky ; writer and revolutionist.* 64 pp. Ld. Lawrence, 1933.

OSTWALD (H.) : *Maxim Gorky.* Transl. by F. A. Welby. Ld. Heinemann, 1905.

GORODETSKY (Sergey), 1884–.

Poems. (*In*: B. Deutsch and A. Yarmolinsky, *Russian poetry*, 1929.)

Poems. (*In*: P. Selver, *Anthology of modern Slavonic literature*, 1919.)

GREBENSHCHIKOV (Georgiy Dmitrievich), 1882–.

The turbulent giant; an epic novel on Russian peasantry. 392 pp. Southbury, Conn. Alatas Publishing Co., 1940.

GRIBOEDOV (Aleksandr Sergeevich), 1795–1829.

The mischief of being clever. Transl. by B. Pares. With introduction by D. S. Mirsky. Published by The School of Slavonic Studies. Ld. Eyre & Spottiswoode, n.d. 68 pp. (Masterpieces of the Slavonic Literature.)

—— Same. With title : *The misfortune of being clever.* Transl. by S. W. Pring. Ld. Nutt, 1914.

—— Same. With title : *Wit works woe.* Transl. by B. Pares. (*In*: G. R. Noyes, *Masterpieces of the Russian drama*, 1933.)

Biography, criticism, etc. :

TYNYANOV (Y. N.) : *Death and diplomacy in Persia.* Transl. by A. Brown. Ld. Boriswood, 1938. [Historical novel on Griboedov.]

GRIGOROVICH (Dmitri Vasilevich), 1822–1900.

The fisherman. Transl. by A. S. Rappoport. Philadelphia. McKay, 1916.

GRINBERG (I.), *See* : BRAMM (M.) and GRINBERG (I.)

GROSSMAN (Vassili).
>   *In the town of Berdichev.* (*In:* J. Rodker, *Soviet anthology*, 1943.)
>   *The people immortal; a novel of the Red Army in action.* 120 pp.
>   Ld. Hutchinson, 1943.

GUL (Roman Borisovich).
>   *Provocateur; a historical novel of the Russian terror.* Authorised
>   transl. by L. Zarine. Ed. by S. Graham. 332 pp. N.Y.
>   Harcourt, 1931.
>   —— Same. With title: *General B. O.* Transl. by L. Zarine.
>   332 pp. Ld. Benn, 1932.

GUMILEV (Nikolay Stefanovich), 1886–1921.
>   Poems. (*In:* C. M. Bowra, *A book of Russian verse*, 1943.)
>   Poems. (*In:* C. F. Coxwell, *Russian poems*, 1929.)
>   Poems. (*In:* G. Reavey and M. Slonim, *Soviet Literature*, 1933.)

GUSEV-ORENBURGSKI (Sergey Ivanovich), 1867–.
>   *The land of the children.* Transl. by N. N. Selivanova. 421 pp.
>   N.Y. Longmans, 1928.
>   —— Same. Cheap ed. 1931.
>   *The land of the fathers.* Transl. by N. N. Selivanova. 298 pp.
>   Ld. Cape, 1925.

HERMAN (Yuri Pavlovich). *See:* GERMAN (Yuri Pavlovich).

HERTSEN (Aleksandr Ivanovich), 1812–70.
>   *Memoirs*, pts. 1–2. Transl. by J. D. Duff. Ld. Oxf. Univ. Pr.,
>   1923.
>   *My past and thoughts: the memoirs of Alexander Herzen.*
>   Transl. by C. Garnett. 6 vols. Ld. Chatto & Windus,
>   1924–27.

>   Biography, criticism, etc.:
>   CARR (E. H.): *The romantic exiles.* 391 pp. Ld. Gollancz, 1933.
>   [Deals with the life of Hertsen, Bakunin and their circle.]

HIPPIUS (Zinaida Nikolaevna) [Mme Merezhkovsky], 1867–.
>   *The green ring;* a play. Transl. by S. S. Koteliansky. Ld.
>   Daniel, 1920.
>   Poems. (*In:* C. F. Coxwell, *Russian poems*, 1929.)
>   Poems. (*In:* B. Deutsch and A. Yarmolinsky, *Russian poetry*,
>   1929.)
>   Poems. (*In:* P. Selver, *Modern Russian poetry*, 1917.)

HODASEVICH (Vladislav). *See:* KHODASEVICH (Vladislav).

ILENKOV (Vasiliy Pavlovich).
>   *Driving axle; a novel of socialist construction.* 455 pp. Ld.
>   Lawrence, 1934.
>   *White mittens.* (*In:* I. Montagu and H. Marshall, *Soviet short
>   stories*, 1944.)

ILF (Ilya Arnoldovich), 1897–1937, and PETROV (Evgeny), –1942.
 Diamonds to sit on: a Russian comedy of errors. Transl. by E.
 Hill and D. Mudie. 280 pp. Ld. Methuen, 1930.
 *Little golden America; two famous Soviet humorists survey these
 U.S.* 387 pp. Ill. N.Y. Farrar, 1937.
 Little golden calf; a satiric novel. Transl. by C. Malamuth. With
 an introduction by A. V. Lunacharsky. 402 pp. Ld.
 Grayson, 1932.
 —— Same. Cheap ed. 384 pp. 1933.
ILIN (Mikhail Andreevich) [pseud. Mikhail Ossorgin], 1878–.
 My sister's story. 235 pp. N.Y. Dial Pr., 1931.
 —— Same. Transl. by N. Helstein and G. Harris. 238 pp.
 Ld. Secker, 1932.
 Quiet Street. Transl. by N. Helstein. 344 pp. Ld. Secker; N.Y.
 Dial Pr., 1930.
ISBACH (Aleksandr), 1904–.
 Duty. (*In:* I. Montagu and H. Marshall, *Soviet short stories,*
 1943.)
 The parcel. (*In:* I. Montagu and H. Marshall, *Soviet short
 stories,* 1942.)
IVANOV (Vsevelod Vyacheslavovich), 1895–.
 Adventures of a fakhir. Abbreviated transl. 300 pp. N.Y.
 Vanguard Pr., 1935.
 —— Same. With title: *Patched breeches.* Toronto. Macmillan.
 —— Same. With title: *I live a queer life: an extraordinary
 autobiography.* 317 pp. Ld. Dickson, 1936.
 —— Same. Extract, with title: *When I was a fakhir.* (*In:* J.
 Cournos, *Short stories out of Soviet Russia,* 1929.)
 Armoured train 14–69; a play in eight scenes. Transl. by Gibson-
 Cowan and A. T. K. Grant. 59 pp. Ld. Lawrence, 1933.
 The baby. (*In:* J. J. Robbins and J. Kunitz, *Azure cities,* 1929.)
 The child. (*In:* J. Cournos, *Short stories out of Soviet Russia,*
 1929.)
 The desert of Tubskoy. (*Extract in :* G. Reavey and M. Slonim,
 Soviet literature, 1933.)
 Unfrozen water. (*In:* S. Konovalov, *Bonfire,* 1932.)
IVANOV (Vyacheslav), 1866–.
 Poems. (*In:* C. M. Bowra, *A book of Russian verse,* 1943.)
 Poems. (*In:* C. F. Coxwell, *Russian poems,* 1929.)
 Poems. (*In:* B. Deutsch and A. Yarmolinsky, *Russian poetry,*
 1929.)
 Poems. (*In:* P. Selver, *Anthology of modern Slavonic literature,*
 1919.)

KALLINIKOV (Josif), 1890–.
  Land of bondage. Transl. by P. Kirwin. 128 pp. Ld. Grayson,
    1931.
  Women and monks. Transl. by P. Kirwin. 873 pp. Ld. Secker;
    N.Y. Harcourt, 1930.
KASSIL (Lev Abramovich), 1905–.
  Land of Shvanbrania : a novel with maps, a coat of arms and a flag.
    Transl. by S. Glass and N. Guterman. 289 pp. N.Y.
    Viking Pr., 1935.
  One quarter of an hour. (*In :* I. Montagu and H. Marshall, *Soviet
    short stories,* 1943.)
  On the captain's bridge. (*In: Mayakovsky and his poetry,*
    1942.)
  The story of Alesha Ryazan and Uncle White Sea. 46 pp. N.Y.
    Co-operative Publ. Society, 1935. [Story for children.]
KATAEV (Valentin Petrovich), 1897–.
  The embezzlers. Transl. by L. Zarine. With introduction by S.
    Graham. 300 pp. N.Y. Dial Pr., 1929; 254 pp. Ld.
    Black, 1929; Ld. Benn, 1930.
  Fellow countrymen. Transl. by J. Cournos. (*In:* J. Cournos,
    Short stories out of Soviet Russia, 1929.)
  —— Same. Repr. in : *Russian short stories,* 1943.
  The golden pen. (*In:* G. Reavey and M. Slonim, *Soviet literature,*
    1933.)
  How he stood the test. (*In:* S. Konovalov, *Bonfire,* 1932.)
  The infant. Transl. by S. Garry. (*In:* J. Rodker, *Soviet
    anthology,* 1943.)
  Knives. Transl. by A. Brown. (Ibid.)
  Peace is where the tempests blow. Transl. by C. Malamuth.
    341 pp. Toronto. Farrar, 1937.
  —— Same. With title : *Lonely white sail; or Peace is where the
    tempests blow.* 341 pp. Ld. Allen, 1937.
  Squaring the circle. Transl. by N. Goold-Verschoyle and adapted
    for Engl. performance. 111 pp. Ld. Wishart, 1934.
  —— Same. Mercury Theatre version : a farce in three acts.
    Rev. by A. Dukes. N.Y. Baker, 1935.
  —— Same. A play in three acts. Transl. and adapted by E.
    Lyons and C. Malamuth. (*In:* E. Lyons, *Six Soviet plays,*
    1935.)
  Things. Transl. by L. Zarine. (*In:* S. Graham, *Great Russian
    short stories,* 1929.)
  Time, forward! Authorised transl. by C. Malamuth. 345 pp.
    Toronto. Farrar, 1933.

—— Same. With title: *Forward, oh Time!* 432 pp. Ld. Gollancz, 1935.

—— Same. (*Extract in:* G. Reavey and M. Slonim, *Soviet literature,* 1933.)

KAVERIN (Veniamin Aleksandrovich), 1902–.

The anonymous artist. (*Extract in:* G. Reavey and M. Slonim, *Soviet literature,* 1933.)

The larger view. Transl. by E. L. Swan. 484 pp. N.Y. Stackpole; Ld. Cassell, 1938. Repr. Cheap ed. Ld. Cassell, 1940.

The last night. (*In:* I. Montagu and H. Marshall, *Soviet short stories,* 1944.)

The return of the Kirghiz. (*From the prologue in:* G. Reavey and M. Slonim, *Soviet literature,* 1933.)

A simple lad. (*In:* I. Montagu and H. Marshall, *Soviet short stories,* 1944.)

Thomas the ostrich. Transl. by S. Garry. (*In:* J. Rodker, *Soviet anthology,* 1943.)

Three meetings. (*In:* I. Montagu and H. Marshall, *Soviet short stories,* 1944.)

Two captains. Transl. by E. L. Swan. 484 pp. Ld. Cassell, 1938; 442 pp. N.Y. Modern Age, 1942.

KAZIN (Vasiliy), 1898–.

The heavenly factory. (*In:* G. Z. Patrick, *Popular poetry in Soviet Russia,* 1929.)

Poems. (*In:* C. M. Bowra, *A book of Russian verse,* 1943.)

Poems. (*In:* B. Deutsch and A. Yarmolinsky, *Russian poetry,* 1929.)

KERASH (Tembot).

Trial by elders. (*In:* I. Montagu and H. Marshall, *Soviet short stories,* 1942.)

KHLEBNIKOV (Velemir), 1885–.

The image of rebellion. (From LEF, in: G. Reavey and M. Slonim, *Soviet literature,* 1933.)

KHODASEVICH (Vladislav), 1886–1938.

Poems. (*In:* C. M. Bowra, *A book of Russian verse,* 1943.)

Poems. (*In: New Directions in prose and poetry,* pp. 535, 1941.)

KHOMYAKOV (Aleksey Stepanovich), 1804–60.

Poem. (*In:* C. M. Bowra, *A book of Russian verse,* 1943.)

Poem. (*In:* C. F. Coxwell, *Russian poems,* 1929.)

KIRSANOV (Semjen), 1906

Poems. (*In: New Directions,* 1941.)

KIRSHON (Vladimir Mikhailovich), 1902–.
> Bread; a play in five acts and nine scenes. Transl. by S. Volochova.
> (In: E. Lyons, Six Soviet plays, 1935.)

KIRSHON (V. M.) and USPENSKIY (Andrey Vasilevich).
> Red rust. Transl. by V. and F. Vernon. 182 pp. N.Y.
> Brentano's, 1930.

KLUCHANSKY (Anna M.).
> Commissar Krilenko. N.Y. Liveright, 1939.

KLUYEV (Nikolay), 1889–.
> Poems. (In: B. Deutsch and A. Yarmolinsky, Modern Russian
> poetry, 1923.)
> Poems. (In: G. Z. Patrick, Popular poetry in Soviet Russia, 1929.)
> Poems. (In: G. Shelley, Modern poems from Russia, 1942.)

KNORRE (Fedor).
> In the dark. (In: I. Montagu and H. Marshall, Soviet short
> stories, 1944.)

KOCHERGA (Ivan).
> Masters of Time; a play in four acts. Transl. by A. Wixley. (In:
> B. Blake, Four Soviet plays, 1937.) [Russian title: The
> watchmaker and the hen.]

KOCHKUROV (Nikolay Ivanovich). See: VESELY (Artem), pseud.

KOLLONTAI (Aleksandra Mikhailovna), 1872–.
> Free love. Transl. by C. J. Hogarth. 279 pp. Ld. Dent, 1934.
> (Dent's Popular Modern Fiction.)
> —— Same. With title: Great love. Transl. by L. Lore. 243 pp.
> N.Y. Vanguard Pr., 1929.
> —— Same. With title: Red love. 286 pp. N.Y. Seven Arts
> Publishing Co., 1927.

KOLTSOV (Aleksey Vasilevich), 1808–42.
> Poems. (In: C. M. Bowra, A book of Russian verse, 1943.)
> Poems. (In: F. Cornford and E. P. Salaman, Poems from the
> Russian, 1943.)
> Poems. (In: C. F. Coxwell, Russian poems, 1929.)
> Poems. (In: B. Deutsch and A. Yarmolinsky, Russian poetry,
> 1929.)
> Poems. (In: P. E. Matheson, Holy Russia, 1917.)

KORNEICHUK (Aleksandr), 1910–.
> The front. (In: Four Soviet war plays, 1943.)
> Guerillas of the Ukrainian steppes. (Ibid.)

KOROLENKO (Vladimir Galaktionovich), 1853–1921.
> Birds of heaven, and other stories. Transl. by C. A. Manning.
> N.Y. Duffield, 1919.
> The blind musician. Transl. by J. W. Luco. N.Y. 1915.

In a strange land. Transl. by G. Zilboorg. 214 pp. N.Y. Richards, 1925.

Makar's dream. Transl. by M. Fell. N.Y. Duffield, 1916.

—— Same. (*In:* S. Graham, *Great Russian short stories,* 1929.)

The murmuring forest, and other stories. Transl. by M. Fell. Ld. Duckworth; N.Y. Duffield, 1916. [Contains: 'The murmuring forests'; 'Makar's dream'; 'In bad company'; 'The day of atonement'.]

KOSSATCH (Larissa Petrovna). *See:* UKRAINKA (Lesya) [pseud.]

KOZHEVNIKOV (Vadim).

The girl who led the way. (*In:* I. Montagu and H. Marshall, *Soviet short stories,* 1944.)

March–April. (*In:* E. Fen, *Soviet stories of the last decade,* 1945.)

The scout. (*In:* I. Montagu and H. Marshall, *Soviet short stories,* 1944.)

KRAVCHINSKY (Sergey M.). *See:* STEPNIAK (Sergey) [pseud. of Sergey M. Kravchinsky.]

KROPOTKIN (Prince Petr Alekseevich), 1842–1921.

Memoirs of a revolutionist. 502 pp. N.Y. Houghton, 1930. (Riverside Library Series.)

Selections from his writings. Ed. with an introduction by H. Read. 150 pp. N.Y. Universal Distributors, 1942; Ld. Freedom Pr., 1943.

KRYLOV (Ivan Andreevich), 1768–1844.

Fables. Transl. into Engl. verse, with a preface, by B. Pares. Ld. Cape, 1926; 271 pp. N.Y. Harcourt, 1927.

—— Same. *Selections, with Russian text.* 88 pp. Ld. Penguin Books, 1942.

—— Same. With title: *Fables from the Russian.* Adapted by S. Mead. 16 pp. Oxf. 1943. (Chameleon series, No. 23.)

Poems. (*In:* F. Cornford and E. P. Salaman, *Poems from the Russian,* 1943.)

Poems. (*In:* C. F. Coxwell, *Russian poems,* 1929.)

KUNINA (Irina) pseud. *See:* ALEKSANDER (Irina).

KUPRIN (Aleksandr Ivanovich), 1870–1938.

The bracelet of garnets, and other stories. Transl. by L. Pasvolsky. Ld. Duckworth; N.Y. Scribner, 1919. [Contains: 'The bracelet of garnets'; 'The horse thieves'; 'The Jewess'; 'Anathema'; 'The Laestrygonians'.]

The duel. Anon. transl. Ld. Allen & Unwin; N.Y. Macmillan, 1916.

Gambrinus, and other stories. Transl. by B. G. Guerney. N.Y. Adelphi, 1926. [Contains: 'Gambrinus'; 'Monte Carlo'; 'Roach hole'.]

In honour's name. Transl. by W. F. Harvey. Ld. Everett, 1907.

Olessia; a novel. Transl. by A. E. Harrison. Ld. Sisley, 1909.

The river of life, and other stories. Transl. by S. S. Koteliansky and J. M. Murry. Ld. Maunsell; Boston. Luce, 1916. [Contains: 'The river of life'; 'Captain Ribnikov'; 'The outrage'; 'The witch'.]

—— Same. New ed. 248 pp. Ld. Allen & Unwin, 1943.

Sasha, and other stories. Transl. by D. Ashby. Ld. Stanley Paul, 1920; Philadelphia. McKay, 1928.

Shulamite. N.Y. Luce, 1915.

Sulamith. Transl. by B. G. Guerney. N.Y. Adelphi, 1926.

A Slav soul, and other stories. Transl. by S. Graham. Ld. Constable, 1916. [Contains: 'A Slav soul'; 'Captain Ribnikov'; 'Mechanical justice'; 'The song and the dance'; 'Tempting providence'.]

Yama. A novel in three pts. Transl. by B. G. Guerney. 447 pp. N.Y. B. G. Guerney, 1929; 340 pp. Ld. Hamilton, 1935.

KUZMIN (Mikhail A.), 1877–.

Poems. (*In:* C. F. Coxwell, *Russian poems*, 1929.)

Poems. (*In:* B. Deutsch and A. Yarmolinsky, *Russian poetry*, 1929.)

LANDAU (Mark Aleksandrovich). *See:* ALDANOV (Mark) pseud.

LAVRENOV (Boris), 1894–.

The old woman. (*In:* I. Montagu and H. Marshall, *Soviet short stories*, 1944.)

LENCH (Leonid).

Russian hospitality. Transl. by A. Brown. (*In:* J. Rodker, *Soviet anthology*, 1943.)

LEONOV (Leonid Maksimovich), 1899–.

By the bonfire. (*In:* S. Konovalov, *Bonfire*, 1932.)

The invasion. (*In: Four Soviet war plays*, 1943.)

Ivan's misadventure. Transl. by J. Cournos. (*In:* J. Cournos, *Short stories out of Soviet Russia*, 1929.) (*Repr. in: Russian short stories*, 1943.)

Road to the ocean. Transl. by N. Guterman. 510 pp. N.Y L. B. Fischer, 1944.

Skutarevsky. Transl. by A. Brown. 444 pp. N.Y. Harcourt; Ld. Dickson, 1936.

—— Same. (*Extract in:* G. Reavey and M. Slonim, *Soviet literature*, 1933.)

Sot. Transl. by I. Montagu and S. S. Nolbandov. With a preface by M. Gorky. 387 pp. Ld. Putnam, 1931.
—— Same. With title: *Soviet river.* 382 pp. N.Y. Dial Pr., 1932.
The thief. Authorised transl. by H. Butler. 566 pp. Ld. Secker, 1931.
Three tales. (*In:* E. Fen, *Modern Russian stories,* 1943.)
The town of Gogulev. (*In:* S. Konovalov, *Bonfire,* 1932.)
Tuatamur. Transl. by I. Montagu and S. S. Nolbandov. 50 pp. Ld. Collet's Bookshop, 1935.

LERMONTOV (Mikhail Yurevich), 1814–41.
Ashib Kerib. (*In:* A. E. Chamot, *Selected Russian short stories,* 1925. World's Classics.)
The demon. Transl. by E. Richter. A literal transl. in the metre of the original. 52 pp. Ld. Nutt, 1910.
—— Same. Transl. by R. Burness. 50 pp. Edinburgh. Douglas & Foulis, 1918.
—— Same. Transl. by G. Shelley, with an introduction by D. S. Mirsky. 56 pp. Ld. Richards Pr., 1930.
Elegy on the death of Pushkin. Transl. by R. Hillyer. (*In:* S. H. Cross and E. J. Simmons, *Centennial essays for Pushkin,* 1937.)
A hero of our time. Transl. by R. Merton, with a foreword by D. S. Mirsky. 247 pp. Ld. Allan, 1928.
—— Same. 265 pp. N.Y. Knopf, 1924. (Borzoi Pocket Books.)
—— Same. With title: *The heart of a Russian.* Transl. by J. H. Wisdom and M. Murray. Ld. Herbert & Daniel, 1912. [Erroneously described in the preface as the first Engl. transl.]
—— Same. With title: *A hero of our own times.* Transl. by E. and C. Paul, for the Lermontoff centenary. 283 pp. Ld. Allen & Unwin, 1940.
—— Same. With title: *A hero of nowadays.* Transl. by J. S. Phillimore. Ld. Nelson, 1924.
—— Same. With title: *Modern hero.* With Engl. transl. and biographical sketch by I. Nestor-Schnurmann. N.Y. Macmillan, n.d.
Poems. (*In:* C. M. Bowra, *A book of Russian verse,* 1943.)
Poems. (*In:* F. Cornford and E. P. Salaman, *Poems from the Russian,* 1943.)
Poems. (*In:* C. F. Coxwell, *Russian poems,* 1929.)
Poems. (*In:* J. Krup, *Six poems from the Russian.* 317 pp. N.Y. The Translator, 1936.)

Poems of Michael Lermontoff. The Russian text with Engl. verse transl., introduction, notes, biography and glossary by E. N. Steinhart. 36 pp. Ld. Paul, Trench, Trubner, 1917.

A sheaf from Lermontov. Transl. by J. J. Robbins. N.Y. Lieber & Lewis, 1923.

Six lyrics from the Ruthenian of Taras Shevchenko ; also *The song of the merchant Kalashnikov, from the Russian of Lermontov,* rendered into Engl. verse by E. L. Voynich. 63 pp. Ld. E. Matthews, 1911.

A song about Tsar Ivan Vasilevich, his young bodyguard and the valiant merchant Kalashnikov. Transl. by J. Cournos, with decorations by P. Nash. Ld. Aquila Pr., 1929.

The testament. Transl. by M. Baring. (*In : The Oxford Book of Russian verse,* 1924.)

—— Same. (*Repr. in :* M. Baring, *Have you anything to declare ?* Ld. Heinemann, 1936.)

Biography, criticism, etc. :

HEIFETZ (A.) : *Lermontov in English ; a list of works by and about the poet.* 18 pp. (*Bulletin of the N.Y. Public Library,* Sept. 1942.)

OSBOURNE (E. A.) : *Early translations from the Russian, 3 : Lermontov.* (*Bookman.* Ld., 1932.)

LESKOV (Nikolay Semenovich), 1831–95.

Cathedral folk. Transl. by I. F. Hapgood. N.Y. Knopf; Ld. Lane (U.S.A. printed), 1924. [The second pt. of a trilogy.]

The enchanted wanderer. Transl. by A. G. Pashkoff. Ld. Jarrolds, 1926.

The musk-ox, and other tales. Transl. by R. Norman. 208 pp. Ld. Routledge, 1944. [Contains : 'Kotin and Platonida'; 'The spirit of Mme Genlis' ; 'The stinger' ; 'A flaming patriot' ; 'The clothes-mender' ; 'The devilchase' ; 'The Alexandrite'.]

The sentry, and other stories. Transl. by A. E. Chamot. Ld. Lane ; N.Y. Knopf, 1922.

Steel flea. Adapted from the Russian by B. Deutsch and A. Yarmolinsky. 64 pp. N.Y. Harper, 1943.

LIBEDINSKY (Yury), 1898–.

A letter. (*In :* S. Konovalov, *Bonfire,* 1932.)

A week. Transl. by A. Ransome. 160 pp. Ld. Allen & Unwin, 1923.

LIDIN (Vladimir) [pseud. of Vladimir Germanovich Gomberg), 1894–.

The apostate. Transl. by H. C. Matheson. 336 pp. Ld. Cape, 1931.

—— Same. With title: *The price of life.* [The Russian title.] N.Y. Harper, 1932.

Glaciers. (*In :* J. Cournos, *Short stories out of Soviet Russia,* 1929.)

Hamlet. (*In :* I. Montagu and H. Marshall, *Soviet short stories,* 1942.)

Harps. (*In :* S. Konovalov, *Bonfire,* 1932.)

The master cook. (*In :* E. Fen, *Soviet stories of the last decade,* 1945.)

Youth. (*In :* J. J. Robbins and J. Kunitz, *Azure cities,* 1929.)

LUGOVSKOY (Vladimir Aleksandrovich), 1901–.

Poems. (*In :* New Directions in prose and poetry, 1941, pp. 543.)

LUKASH (Ivan Sozontovich).

The flames of Moscow. Transl. by N. Duddington. 475 pp. N.Y. Macmillan, 1930.

LUNACHARSKY (Anatoly Vasilevich), 1876–1933.

The bear's wedding. Transl. by L. Zamkovsky and N. Borudin. Ld. 1926.

Three plays. Transl. by L. A. Magnus and K. Walter. 299 pp. Ld. Routledge, 1923. (Broadway Translations.) [Contains : 'Faust and the city' ; 'Vasilisa the wise' ; 'The magi'.]

LUNTS (Lev Nataovich), 1901–24.

The city of truth ; a play in three acts. Transl. by J. Silver. 52 pp. Ld. 1929.

MAKARENKO (Anton Semenovich), 1888–.

The road to life. [Autobiography.] Transl. by S. Garry. 287 pp. Ld. Drummond, 1936.

The road to life : the story of the Gorky colony. Transl. by S. Garry. 287 pp. Ld. Drummond, 1938.

MALYSHKIN (Aleksandr Georgievich), 1890–.

South-bound. (*In :* E. Fen, *Soviet stories of the last decade,* 1945.)

MANDELSTAM (Osip E.), 1892–.

Poem. (*In :* C. F. Coxwell, *Russian poems,* 1929.)

Poems. (*In :* C. M. Bowra, *A book of Russian verse,* 1943.)

MATVEEV (Vladimir).

Bitter draught. Transl. by D. Flower. 297 pp. Ld. Cassell, 1935.

Commissar of the Gold Express ; an episode in the Civil War. 212 pp. Ld. Lawrence, 1933 ; N.Y. International Publishers Co., 1933.

MAYAKOVSKY (Vladimir Vladimirovich), 1894–1930.

'I' ; 'Listen' ; 'The cloud in trousers' ; 'Brother writers' ; 'Command no. 1' ; 'Hands off China'. (*In :* G. Reavey and M. Slonim, *Soviet literature,* 1933.)

Mayakovsky and his poetry. Compiled by H. Marshall. Ld. Pilot Pr., 1942. (Life and Literature in the Soviet Union, 3.) [Contains: Report of Mayakovsky's twentieth anniversary exhibition, and other material concerning Mayakovsky.]

Mystery-Bouffe. Transl. by G. R. Noyes and A. S. Kaun. (*In:* G. R. Noyes, *Masterpieces of the Russian drama,* 1933.)

Our march. Transl. by J. Freeman. (*In:* J. Freeman and others, *Voices of October,* 1930.)

Poems. (*In:* C. M. Bowra, *A book of Russian verse,* 1943.)

Poems. (*In:* C. F. Coxwell, *Russian poems,* 1929.)

Poems. (*In:* B. Deutsch and A. Yarmolinsky, *Modern Russian poetry,* 1923, and in their: *Russian poetry,* 1929.)

Poems. (*In: New Directions, anthology in prose and poetry,* 1941, pp. 605–18.)

Biography, criticism, etc.:

DRAKE (W. A.): *Contemporary European writers.* 408 pp. Ld. Harrap. (U.S.A. printed), 1929. [Contains: a chapter on Mayakovsky.]

MAYKOV (Apollon Nikolaevich), 1821–98.

Poems. (*In:* C. M. Bowra, *A book of Russian verse,* 1943.)

Poems. (*In:* F. Cornford and E. P. Salaman, *Poems from the Russian,* 1943.)

Poems. (*In* C. F. Coxwell, *Russian poems,* 1929.)

MEREZHKOVSKY (Dmitri Sergeevich), 1865–1941.

Akhnaton, king of Egypt. Transl. by N. A. Duddington. 372 pp. N.Y. Dutton, 1927.

Birth of the gods. Transl. by N. A. Duddington. 233 pp. Ld. Dent, 1926.

Death of the gods. Transl. by H. Trench. N.Y. Putnam, n.d.

December the fourteenth; a novel. Transl. by N. A. Duddington. 319 pp. Ld. Cape, 1925.

Jesus the unknown. Transl. by E. N. Matheson. N.Y. Scribner, 1934.

—— Same. With title: *Jesus manifest.* Transl. by E. Gellibrand. N.Y. Scribner, 1936.

Julian Apostate. Transl. by B. G. Guerney. N.Y. Modern Library Co., 1929.

The life work of Calderon, etc. Transl. by G. A. Mounsey. 1908–12.

Menace of the mob. Transl. by B. G. Guerney. N.Y. Frank Maurice, 1926.

Michael Angelo, and other sketches. Transl. by N. A. Duddington. 184 pp. Ld. Dent, 1930. [Contains: 'Michael Angelo'; 'Love is stronger than death'; 'Science of love'.]

My life. (*In:* P. Selver, *Anthology of modern Slavonic literature,* 1919.)

Peter and Alexis, the romance of Peter the Great. N.Y. Putnam, n.d.

Poems. (*In:* P. Selver, *Anthology of modern Slavonic literature,* 1919.)

The romance of Leonardo da Vinci. Transl. by H. Trench. N.Y. Putnam, 1924.

—— Same. Transl. by B. G. Guerney. N.Y. Modern Library Co., 1928.

—— Same. With 100 reproductions of the work of Leonardo da Vinci. 580 pp. Ld. Faber, 1938.

—— Same. With title: *Forerunner: the romance of Leonardo da Vinci.* Ld. Constable, 1938.

The secret of the West. Done into Engl. by J. Cournos. 449 pp. Ld. Cape, 1936.

Tolstoy as man and artist, with an essay on Dostoevsky. Ld. Constable, 1902. [Abr. transl. of Tolstoy and Dostoevsky.]

MEREZHKOVSKY (Mme). *See:* HIPPIUS (Zinaida Nikolaevna) [Mme Merezhkovsky.]

MINSKY (N. M.) [pseud. of Nikolay Vilenkin], 1855–.

Poems. (*In:* C. F. Coxwell, *Russian poems,* 1929.)

Poems. (*In:* B. Deutsch and A. Yarmolinsky, *Russian poetry,* 1929.)

Poems. (*In:* P. Selver, *Anthology of modern Slavonic literature,* 1919.)

NABOKOV (Vladimir Vladimirovich) [pseud. Serin], 1899–.

Despair. Transl. by the author. 286 pp. Ld. Long, 1937.

NADSON (Semen Yakovlevich), 1862–87.

Poems. (*In:* C. F. Coxwell, *Russian poems,* 1929.)

Poems. (*In:* P. E. Matheson, *Holy Russia,* 1917.)

NAZAROV (Pavel Szepanovich).

Moved on! from Kashgar to Kashmir. Rendered into Engl. by M. Burr. 317 pp. Ill. Ld. Allen, 1935.

NAZHIVIN (Ivan Fedorovich), 1874–.

According to Thomas; an historical novel of the first century. Transl. by E. Burns. 397 pp. N.Y. Harper, 1931.

The dogs. 336 pp. N.Y. Lippincott, 1931; Ld. Allen & Unwin.

Rasputin. Transl. by C. J. Hogarth. 2 vols. N.Y. Knopf, 1929.

NEKRASOV (Nikolay Alekseevich), 1821–77.
> Poems. Transl. by J. M. Soskice. With an introduction by
> Lascelles Abercrombie. Ld. Oxf. Univ. Pr., 1929. (World's
> Classics.)
> Poems. (*In*: C. M. Bowra, *A book of Russian verse*, 1943.)
> Poems. (*In*: F. Cornford and E. P. Salaman, *Poems from the
> Russian*, 1943.)
> Poems. (*In*: C. F. Coxwell, *Russian poems*, 1929.)
> Poems. (*In*: B. Deutsch and A. Yarmolinsky, *Russian poetry*,
> 1929.)
> Poems. (*In*: O. Elton, *Verse from Pushkin and others*, 1935.)
> Poems. (*In*: N. Jarintsov, *Russian poets and poems*, 1917.)
> Poems. (*In*: P. E. Matheson, *Holy Russia*, 1917.)

NEMIROVICH-DANCHENKO (Vasiliy Ivanovich), 1848–.
> *My life in the Russian theatre.* Transl. by J. Cournos. 358 pp.
> Ld. Bles, 1936.
> *Peasant tales of Russia.* Transl. by C. Field. Ld. Scott, 1917.
> *The princes of the stock exchange.* Transl. by A. S. Rappoport.
> Ld. Holden & Hardingham, 1914.
> *With a diploma* and *The whirlwind.* Transl. by W. J. S. Pyper.
> N.Y. Luce, 1915.

NEVEROV (Aleksandr) [pseud. of Aleksandr Sergeevich Skobolov],
1886–1923.
> *Andron the good-for-nothing.* (*In*: E. Fen, *Modern Russian
> stories*, 1943.)
> *Marya, the Bolshevik.* (*In*: J. J. Robbins and J. Kunitz, *Azure
> cities*, 1929.)
> *Tashkent.* Transl. by R. Merton and W. G. Walton. 224 pp.
> Ld. Gollancz, 1930.
> ——Same. With title: *City of Bread.* Anon. transl. N.Y.
> Doubleday, 1927.
> ——Same. (*Extract in*: S. Konovalov, Bonfire, 1932).

NIKITIN (Ivan Savich), 1824–61.
> Poems. (*In*: C. F. Coxwell, *Russian poems*, 1929.)
> Poems. (*In*: P. E. Matheson, *Holy Russia*, 1917.)

NOVIKOV-PRIBOY (Aleksey Silich), 1877–.
> *Tsushima.* Trans. by E. and C. Paul. 425 pp. Ld. Allen &
> Unwin, 1936.

ODOEVTSEVA (Irina).
> *Out of childhood.* Transl. and ill. by D. Nachshen. 252 pp. N.Y.
> Smith, 1930; Ld. Constable, 1934.

OGAREV (Nikolay Platonovich), 1813–79.
> Poems. (*In*: C. F. Coxwell, *Russian poems*, 1929.)
> Poems. (*In*: P. E. Matheson, *Holy Russia*, 1917.)

OGNEV (N.) [pseud. of Mikhail Grigorevich Rozanov], 1890–.
Diary of a communist schoolboy. Transl. by A. Werth. 288 pp.
Ld. Gollancz, 1928.
Diary of a communist undergraduate. Transl. by A. Werth.
288 pp. Ld. Gollancz, 1929.
Sour grapes and sweet. (*In:* Penguin New Writing, 1. Ld.
Penguin Books, 1940.)

OKULEV (A.).
The unexpected meeting. (*In:* S. Graham, *Great Russian short
stories,* 1929.)

OLESHA (Yuri Karlovich), 1899–.
The cherry stone. (*In:* G. Reavey and M. Slonim, *Soviet literature,*
1933.)
—— Same. Another transl. (*In:* I. Montagu and H. Marshall,
Soviet short stories, 1942.)
The conspiracy of feelings. (*In:* S. Konovalov, *Bonfire,* 1932.)
Envy. Transl. by A. Wolfe. 275 pp. Ld. Hogarth Pr., 1936.
—— Same. (*Extract in:* S. Konovalov, *Bonfire,* 1932.)
Love. Transl. by A. Wolfe. (*In:* Penguin New Writing, 9. Ld.
Lane, 1942.)

ORENBURGSKI (Sergey Gusev-) [pseud.]. *See:* GUSEV-ORENBURGSKI
(Sergey Ivanovich.)

ORESHIN (Piotr V.), 1887–.
Poems. (*In:* B. Deutsch and A. Yarmolinsky, *Modern Russian
poetry,* 1923.)

OSSORGIN (Mikhail) [pseud.]. *See:* ILIN (Mikhail Andreevich)
[Mikhail Ossorgin, pseud.].

OSTROVSKY (Aleksandr Nikolaevich), 1823–86.
A domestic picture. (*In:* E. L. Voynich, *Humour of Russia,* 1911.)
Easy money, and two other plays. Ld. Allen, c. 1944.
Enough stupidity in every wise man. (*In:* O. M. Sayler, *Moscow
Art Theatre of Russian plays,* second series, 1923.)
The forest. Transl. by C. V. Winslow and G. R. Noyes. 126 pp.
N.Y. French, ·1926. (World's Best Plays by European
Authors.)
Incompatibility of temper. (*In:* E. L. Voynich, *Humour of Russia,*
1911.)
King of comedy [play]. Transl. by J. M. Petrie. 96 pp. Ld.
Stockwell, 1937.
Plays. Transl. and ed. by G. R. Noyes. N.Y. Scribner, 1917.
[Contains: 'A protégé of the mistress'; 'Poverty is no crime';
'Sin and sorrow are common to all'; 'It's a family affair,
we'll settle it ourselves'.]

The poor bride. Transl. by J. L. Seymour and G. R. Noyes. (*In:* G. R. Noyes, *Masterpieces of the Russian drama,* 1933.)

The storm. Transl. by C. Garnett. 120 pp. Chicago. Sergel, 1899 and 1911; Boston. Luce, 1907; Ld. Duckworth, 1899 and 1930.

—— Same; a play in three acts. Engl. version by G. F. Holland and M. Morley. 112 pp. Ld. Allen, 1930. (Plays of Everyman Theatre Guild, no. 1.)

—— Same. With title: *Thunderstorm;* a drama in five acts. Transl. by F. Whyte and G. R. Noyes. 83 pp. N.Y. French, 1927. (World's Best Plays by European Authors.)

We won't brook interference; a farce in two acts. Transl. by J. L. Seymour and G. R. Noyes. 39 pp. San Francisco. Banner, 1938.

OSTROVSKY (Nikolay Alekseevich), 1904–1937.

Born of the storm. Transl. by L. L. Hiler. 251 pp. N.Y. Critics Group, 1939.

Making of a hero. Transl. by A. Brown. 440 pp. Ld. Secker & Warburg, 1938.

OUTKIN (Iosif): Poems. (*In:* New *Directions in prose and poetry,* 1941.)

PANFEROV (Fedor Ivanovich), 1896–.

And then the harvest. Transl. by S. Garry. 457 pp. Ld. Putnam, 1939.

Brusski; a story of peasant life in Soviet Russia. Transl. by Z. Mitrov and J. Tabrisky. 300 pp. Ld. Lawrence, 1931.

PASTERNAK (Boris Leonidovich), 1890–.

Childhood. Transl. by R. Tayne. Singapore. Straits Times Pr., 1941.

The death of a poet. From: *The safe conduct.* (*In:* G. Reavey and M. Slonim, *Soviet literature,* 1933.)

Poems. (*In:* C. M. Bowra, *A book of Russian verse,* 1943.)

Poems. (*In:* C. F. Coxwell, *Russian poems,* 1929.)

Poems. (*In:* G. Reavey and M. Slonim, *Soviet literature,* 1933.)

Poems. (*In:* New *Directions in prose and poetry,* 1941.)

PAVLENKO (Petr Andreevich), 1899–.

Nightpiece. Transl. by S. Garry. (*In:* J. Rodker, *Soviet anthology,* 1943.)

Red 'planes fly east. Transl. by S. Garry. 523 pp. Ld. Routledge, 1938.

PAVLOVA (Caroline), 1820–98.

Poems. (*In:* C. F. Coxwell, *Russian poems,* 1929.)

PAVSTOVSKY (Konstantin).
    The copper plates. (*In:* J. Rodker, *Soviet anthology*, 1943.)
    The razor. (*In:* I. Montagu and H. Marshall, *Soviet short stories*, 1943.)
    The sailmaker. (*In:* I. Montagu and H. Marshall, *Soviet short stories*, 1942.)
PERELMAN (O. I.). *See:* DYMOV (Osip) [pseud. of O. I. Perelman].
PERETZ (Isaac Loeb), 1851–1915.
    Bontshe, the silent. Transl. from the Yiddish with preface and glossary by A. S. Rappoport. 259 pp. McKay, n.d.
    One-act plays from the Yiddish, by I. L. Peretz and others. Transl. by E. Block. 123 pp. N.Y., 1929.
    Stories and pictures. Transl. from the Yiddish by H. Frank. Philadelphia. Jewish Publ., 1906.
  Biography, criticism, etc.:
    ROBACK (A. A.): *I. L. Peretz, psychologist of literature.* N.Y. Science and Art Publ., 1935.
PERVENTSEV (Arkady).
    Cossack commander. Transl. by S. Garry. 313 pp. Ld. Routledge, 1939.
PESHKOV (Aleksey Maksimovich). *See:* GORKY (Maksim) [pseud. of Aleksey Maksimovich Peshkov.].
PETROV (Evgeny),-1942. *See also:* ILF (Ilya Arnoldovich) and PETROV (Evgeny).
    The professor of music. (*In:* I. Montagu and H. Marshall, *Soviet short stories*, 1943.)
PETROV (Stepan Gavrilovich). *See:* Skitalets, [pseud. of Stepan Gavrilovich Petrov].
PILNYAK (Boris) [pseud. of Boris Andreevich Vogau], 1894–.
    His majesty Kneeb Piter Komondor. (*In:* S. Graham, *Great Russian short stories*, 1929.)
    The human mind. (*In:* J. Cournos, *Short stories out of Soviet Russia*, 1932.)
    Ivan Moscow. Transl. by A. S. Schwartzmann. 92 pp. N.Y. Christopher, 1935.
    The law of the wolf [short story]. (*In:* J. J. Robbins and J. Kunitz, *Azure cities*, 1929.)
    The naked year. Transl. by A. Brown. 305 pp. N.Y. Brewer, 1928. [The Russian title: *A bare year.*]
    —— Same. (*Extract in:* S. Konovalov, *Bonfire*, 1932.)
    —— Same. (*Extract in:* G. Reavey and M. Slonim, *Soviet literature*, 1933.)
    —— Same. (*Extract in:* J. Rodker, *Soviet anthology*, 1943.)

Tales of the wilderness. Transl. by F. O. Dempsey. With an introduction by D. S. Mirsky. 223 pp. Ld. Routledge, 1924.

The volga falls to the Caspian sea. Transl. by C. Malamuth. 322 pp. Ld. Davies, 1932.

—— Same. Cheap ed. 1935.

A year of their life. (*In:* E. Fen, *Modern Russian stories,* 1943.)

PISEMSKY (Aleksey Teofilaktovich), 1820–81.

A bitter fate. Transl. by A. Kagan and G. R. Noyes. (*In:* G. R. Noyes, *Masterpieces of the Russian drama,* 1933.)

PLATONOV (A.).

The third son. (*In:* I. Montagu and H. Marshall, *Soviet short stories,* 1942.)

POGODIN (Nikolay Fedorovich), 1900–.

Aristocrats; a comedy in four acts. Transl. by A. Wixley and R. S. Carr. (*In:* B. Blake, *Four Soviet plays,* 1937.)

—— Same. Acting ed. Ld. Lawrence, 1937.

Tempo; a play in four acts. Transl. by I. D. W. Talmadge. (*In:* E. Lyons, *Six Soviet plays,* 1935.)

POLONSKY (Yakov Petrovich), 1819–98.

Poems. (*In:* C. M. Bowra, *A book of Russian verse,* 1943.)

Poems. (*In:* C. F. Coxwell, *Russian poems,* 1929.)

Poems. (*In:* B. Deutsch and A. Yarmolinsky, *Russian poetry,* 1929.)

POPOV (Aleksandr Serafimovich). *See:* SERAFIMOVICH (Aleksandr) [pseud. of Aleksandr Serafimovich Popov].

PRIDVOROV (Yefim Alekseevich). *See:* BEDNY (Demyan) [pseud. of Yefim Alekseevich Pridvorov].

PRISHVIN (Mikhail Mikhailovich), 1873–.

Jen Sheng, the root of life. Engl. version by G. Walton and P. Gibbons. Foreword by J. S. Huxley. 177 pp. Ld. Melrose, 1936.

A werewolf of the steppe. (*In:* J. Cournos, *Short stories out of Soviet Russia,* 1929.)

—— Same. (*Repr. in:* Russian short stories, 1943.)

PUSHKIN (Aleksandr Sergeevich), 1799–1837.

The works of Alexander Pushkin : lyrics, narrative poems, folk tales, plays, prose. Selected and ed. with an introduction by A. Yarmolinsky. 893 pp. N.Y. Random House; Ld. Nonesuch Pr. (Faber), 1936. Contains:

46 lyrical poems and ballads. Transl. by M. Baring, T. B. Shaw, M. Eastman, C. Garnett and B. Deutsch.

Narrative poems: 'Poltava' (from canto 3), transl. by B.

Deutsch; 'The Bronze Horseman', transl. by O. Elton; 'Eugene Onegin', transl. by B. Deutsch.

Folk tales: 'The tale of the Pope and of his workman Balda', transl. by O. Elton; 'The tale of the golden cockerel', transl. by B. Deutsch.

Plays: 'Boris Godunov', transl. by A. Hayes; 'The covetous knight'; 'Mozart and Salieri', and 'The stone guest', transl. by A. F. B. Clark.

Prose: 'The shot'; 'The snowstorm'; 'The undertaker'; 'The postmaster.'; 'The Queen of Spades'; 'Mistress into maid'; 'Kirdjali.' Transl. by T. Keane. 'The captain's daughter', transl. by N. Duddington. 'The negro of Peter the Great'; 'Dubrowsky'; 'Egyptian nights', transl. by T. Keane.

The avaricious knight. Transl. by E. J. Simmons. (Harvard studies and notes in philology and literature. Cambridge, Mass., vol. 15, 1933.)

Boris Godunov. Rendered into Engl. verse by A. Hayes. 117 pp. Ld. Kegan Paul; N.Y. Dutton, 1918.

The captain's daughter, and other stories. Ld. Hodder & Stoughton, 1915.

The captain's daughter, and other tales. Transl. by N. Duddington. Ld. Dent, 1923; N.Y. Dutton, 1935. (Everyman's Library.) [Contains: 'The captain's daughter'; 'The Queen of Spades'; 'Dubrowsky'; 'Peter the Great's negro'; 'The station-master'.]

The captain's daughter. Transl. by N. Duddington, with an introduction by E. Garnett. 212 pp. Ld. Dent, 1928.

Eugene Onegin: a novel in verse. Transl. by D. Prall Radin and G. Z. Patrick. 226 pp. Berkeley. Univ. of California Pr., 1937.
—— Same. Transl. by O. Elton. Ill. With a foreword by D. MacCarthy. Ld. Pushkin Pr., 1937.
—— Same. Ordinary ed. 1939.

The fountain of Bakchesarai. (*Extract in:* L. Wiener, *Anthology of Russian literature*, vol. 2. 1903.)

Gabriel: a poem in one song. Transl. by M. Eastman. Ill. N.Y. Covici, Friede, 1929.

The golden cockerel, from the original Russian fairy tale, by E. Pogany. Ill. 48 pp. U.S.A. 1938; Ld. Nelson, 1939.
—— Same. Rendered into Engl. verse by N. Katkoff. Ld. Beaumont, 1918.
—— Same. With title: *The tale of the golden cockerel.* Transl. by H. Waller. Ill. 22 pp. Ld. Golden Cockerel Pr., 1937, Ltd. ed.

Mozart and Salieri. [Play.] Transl. by A. Werth. (*In: The Glasgow book of prose and verse.* Glasgow. Hodge, 1923.]

Poems. Transl. by M. Baring. Ld. Privately printed, 1931.

Poems. (*In: Bechhofer, A Russian anthology in English,* 1917.)

Poems. (*In: Bowra, A book of Russian verse,* 1943.)

Poems. (*In: Cornford and Salaman, Poems from the Russian,* 1943.)

Poems. (*In: Coxwell, Russian poems,* 1929.)

Poems. (*In: Deutsch and Yarmolinsky, Modern Russian poetry,* 1923, and: *Russian poetry, 1927 and 1929.*)

Poems. (*In: Elton, Verse from Pushkin and others,* 1935.)

Poems. (*In: Jarintsov, Russian poets and poems,* 1917.)

Poems. (*In: Krup, Six poems from the Russian,* 1936.)

Poems. (*In: Matheson, Holy Russia,* 1918.)

Poems. (*In: Pollen, Russian songs and lyrics,* 1917.)

Poems. (*In: Wiener, Anthology of Russian literature,* vol. 2, 1903.)

Poems. (*In: Zeitlin, Skazki: tales and legends of old Russia,* 1926.)

The Queen of Spades. Transl. by R. S. Townsend. (*In his: Short stories by Russian authors,* 1924.)

—— Same. Transl. by A. E. Chamot. (*In his: Selected Russian short stories,* 1925.)

—— Same. Transl. by J. E. Pouterman and C. Bruerton. Introductory essay by D. S. Mirsky. Ill. 110 pp. Ld. Blackamore Pr., 1929.

The Russian wonderland: a metrical translation by B. L. Brasol. 62 pp. Ld. Williams & Norgate, 1936.

Three tales: The snowstorm; The postmaster; The undertaker. Transl. by R. T. Currall. With Russian text. Ld. Harrap, 1919. (Harrap's bilingual series.)

The Zigany. Transl. by G. Borrow. (*In: Borrow, Works,* vol. 16. Ld. Constable, 1924.)

Biography, criticism, etc.:

OSBOURNE (E. A.): *Early translation from the Russian: 2, Pushkin and his contemporaries.* (*Bookman,* vol. 82. Ld. 1932.)

Pushkin in English. A list of works by and about Pushkin. Compiled by the Slavonic division of the New York Public Library. (*Bulletin of the New York Public Library,* July, 1932.)

BARING (M.): *Lost lectures; or the fruits of experience.* Ld. Heinemann, 1932. [Contains: pp. 178–99, essay on Pushkin and transl. of some lyrics.]

BATES (A.): *Russian drama.* Ld. Historical Publishing Co., 1906. [Contains: a short biography of Pushkin and a critical analysis of Boris Godunov and the miniature dramas and fragments.]

BECKWITH (M. W.) and others : *Pushkin the man and artist.* By various authors. 245 pp. Ld. Williams & Norgate; N.Y. Paisley Pr., 1937.

BRASOL (B. L.) : *Poushkin, the Shakespeare of Russia.* [Address delivered before the Brooklyn Institute of Arts and Sciences, 1931.] N.Y. Privately printed, 1931.

CLEUGH (J.) : *Prelude to Parnassus: scenes from the life of A. S. Pushkin.* 342 pp. Ld. Barker, 1936.

CROSS (S. H.) and SIMMONS (E. J.) : *A. Pushkin ; his life and literary heritage.* 79 pp. N.Y. American-Russian Institute for Cultural Relations with the Soviet Union, 1937.

CROSS (S. H.) and SIMMONS (E. J.) ed. : *Centennial essays for Pushkin.* 226 pp. Cambridge, Mass. Harvard Univ. Pr., 1937.

ELTON (O.) : *Alexander Pushkin. (In his: Essays and addresses,* 1939.) [Contains : transl. of several poems by Elton, Baring, R. M. Hewitt, B. Pares.]

HERFORD (C. H.) : *A Russian Shakespearean: a centenary study.* 30 pp. Skemp Memorial Lecture in the University of Bristol, 1925.

—— Same. Enlarged version in his: *The post-war mind of Germany, and other European studies.* 248 pp. Oxf. Clarendon Pr., 1927.

MIRSKY (D. S.) : *Pushkin.* 266 pp. Ld. Routledge, 1926. (Republic of letters.)

Pushkin: a collection of articles and essays. Ed. by M. P. Sokolnikov. 188 pp. Moscow. VOKS, 1939.

TALMADGE (I. D. W.) : *Pushkin; homage by Marxist critics.* Transl. by B. G. Guerney. 104 pp. N.Y. Critics' Group, 1937. [Contains : essays by Gorky, Zeitlin, Lunacharsky, Vinogradov.]

WILSON (E.) : *In honour of Pushkin. (In his: The triple thinkers,* Oxf., 1938.)

RABINOWITZ (Shalom). *See :* ALEICHEM (Shalom) [pseud. of Shalom Rabinowitz].

RASKIN (A.) and SLOBODSKY (M.).
My birthday. Transl. by A. Brown. *(In:* J. Rodker, *Soviet anthology,* 1943.)

REMIZOV (Aleksey Mikhailovich), 1877–.
The clock and *Three prose lyrics from Shumy Goroda.* Transl. by J. Cournos. 222 pp. Ld. Chatto & Windus, 1924.

Fifth pestilence, together with *The history of the tinkling cymbal and sounding brass, Ivan Semyonovich Stratilatov.* Transl.

with a preface by A. Brown. 235 pp. N.Y. Payson & Clarke, 1928.

ROMANOV (Panteleimon Sergeevich), 1884–1936.

Black fritters. (*In :* J. J. Robbins and J. Kunitz, *Azure cities,* 1929.)

Diary of a Soviet marriage : a study of a woman, her husband and the friend. Transl. by J. P. Furnivall and R. Parmenter. Introduction by J. Lavrin. 143 pp. Ld. Nott, 1936.

The new commandment. Transl. by V. Snow. 288 pp. N.Y. Scribner, 1933 ; 341 pp. Ld. Benn, 1933.

—— Same. Cheap ed. Ld. Benn, 1935.

On the Volga, and other stories. Transl. by A. Gretton. 286 pp. Ld. Benn, 1934.

—— Same. Cheap ed. 1936.

The rye cakes. (*In :* S. Konovalov, *Bonfire,* 1932.)

Sex problems. Transl. by E. Fen. (*In her : Modern Russian stories,* 1943.)

Three pairs of silk stockings : a novel of the life of the educated classes under the Soviet. Transl. by L. Zarine. Ed. by S. Graham. 344 pp. Ld. Benn, 1931.

—— Same. Cheap ed. 352 pp. 1932.

White flowers. (*In :* S. Konovalov, *Bonfire,* 1932.)

Without cherry blossom. Transl. by L. Zarine. Ed. by S. Graham. 287 pp. Ld. Benn, 1930.

—— Same. Cheap ed. 1931.

ROONOVA (Olga).

The thief. (*In :* E. Fen, *Soviet stories of the last decade,* 1945.)

ROPSHIN (pseud). *See :* SAVINKOV (Boris Viktorovich).

ROZANOV (Mikhail Grigorevich). *See :* OGNEV (N.) [pseud. of Mikhail Grigorevich Rozanov].

ROZANOV (Vasiliy Vasilevich), 1856–1919.

Fallen leaves. Transl. by S. S. Koteliansky. 166 pp. Ld. Mandrake Pr., 1929.

Solitaria. Transl. by S. S. Koteliansky. With a sketch of the author's life by E. Gollerbach. 188 pp. Ld. Wishart, 1927.

"RUSSIAN BOY".

Russian boy. Fragment of an autobiography from 1916–24. With a glossary 139 pp. Ld. King & Staples, 1942.

SALTYKOV (Mikhail Evgrafovich) [pseud. Shchedrin], 1826–89.

Fables. Transl. by V. Volkhovsky. 257 pp. Ld. Chatto & Windus, 1931. (Phoenix Library.)

The Golovlyov family. Transl. by A. Ridgeway. Ld. 1916.

—— Same. Transl. by N. Duddington. 336 pp. Ld. Allen & Unwin, 1931.

—— Reissued with an introduction by E. Garnett. 324 pp. Ld. Dent, 1934. (Everyman's Library.)

Biography, criticism, etc. :

STRELSKY (N.) : *Saltykov and the Russian Squire.* 176 pp. Oxf., 1940.

SAVINKOV (Boris Viktorovich) [pseud. Ropshin], 1879–1925.

The black horse. Ld. Williams & Norgate, 1924.

Memoirs of a terrorist. Transl. by J. Shaplen. With a foreword and epilogue. 364 pp. N.Y. Boni, 1931.

The pale horse. Transl. by Z. Vengerova. Dublin. Maunsel; Ld. Allen & Unwin, 1917. (Modern Russian Library.)

What never happened. Transl. by T. Seltzer. Ld. Allen & Unwin, 1917.

SCHWARZMAN (Lev Isaakovich). *See :* SHESTOV (Lev) [pseud.].

SEIFULLINA (Lydia Nikolaevna), 1899–.

The law-breakers. (*In :* G. Reavey and M. Slonim, *Soviet literature*, 1933.)

The old woman. (*In :* J. J. Robbins and J. Kunitz, *Azure cities*, 1929.)

SELVINSKY (Ilya Lvovich), 1899–.

The golden melody, from 'Pao-Pao'. (*In :* G. Reavey and M. Slonim, *Soviet literature*, 1933.)

Poems. (*In : New directions in prose and poetry*, 1941, pp. 558–664.)

SEMENOV (Sergey), 1893–.

The birth of a slave. (*In :* S. Konovalov, *Bonfire*, 1932.)

Natalia Tarpova. (*Extract in :* G. Reavey and M. Slonim, *Soviet literature*, 1933.)

SERAFIMOVICH (Aleksandr) [pseud. of Aleksandr Serafimovich Popov), 1863–.

The iron flood. Anon. transl. 246 pp. Ld. Lawrence, 1935.

SERGEEV–TSENSKY (Sergey Nikolaevich), 1876–.

The demigod. (*In :* P. Selver, *Anthology of modern Slavonic literature*, 1919.)

The man you couldn't kill. (*In :* J. Cournos, *Short stories out of Soviet Russia*, 1929.)

—— Same. Repr. in : *Russian short stories*, 1943.

Transfiguration. Transl. by M. Budberg. Ed. with an introduction by M. Gorky. 300 pp. N.Y. MacBride, 1926.

SHAGINYAN (Marietta Sergeevna), 1888–.

Three looms. (*In :* J. J. Robbins and J. Kunitz, *Azure cities*, 1929.)

SHCHEDRIN [pseud.]. *See :* SALTYKOV (Mikhail Evgrafovich).

SHENSHIN. *See :* FET (Afanasy Afanasevich), afterwards Shenshin.

SHESTOV (Lev) [pseud. of Lev Isaakovich Schwarzman), 1866–1938.

All things are possible. Transl. by S. S. Koteliansky. Ld. Secker & Warburg, 1921.

Anton Chekhov, and other essays. Transl. by S. S. Koteliansky and J. M. Murry. Ld. 1916. (Modern Russian Library.)

—— Same. With title: *Penultimate words, and other essays.* 205 pp. N.Y. Luce, 1917.

In Job's balances; on the sources of the eternal truths. Transl. from the German by C. Coventry and C. A. Macartney. 413 pp. Ld. Dent, 1932.

SHEVCHENKO (Taras Grigorevich), 1814–61.

Autobiography. (*In:* P. Selver, *Anthology of modern Slavonic literature,* 1919.)

Poems. (*In:* P. Selver, *Anthology of modern Slavonic literature,* 1919.)

Six lyrics from the Ruthenian of Taras Shevchenko. Also: *The song of the Merchant Kalashnikov from Lermontov,* rendered into Engl. verse, with a biographical sketch, by E. L. Voynich. 63 pp. Ld. Elkin Matthews, 1911.

SHIRYAEV (Petr Alekseevich), 1888–1935.

Flattery's foal. Transl. by A. Fremantle. 295 pp. N.Y. Knopf, 1938. (Borzoi Books.)

—— Same. With title: *Taglioni's grandson; the story of a Russian horse.* 291 pp. Ld. Putnam, 1939.

—— Cheap ed. 1941.

SHISHKOV (Vyacheslav Yakovlevich), 1873–.

Children of darkness. 288 pp. Ld. Gollancz, 1931.

Cranes. [Short story.] (*In:* J. J. Robbins and J. Kunitz, *Azure cities,* 1929).

SHKLOVSKY (Viktor).

St. Petersburg in 1920. (*In:* S. Konovalov, *Bonfire,* 1932.)

SHMELEV (Ivan Sergeevich), 1875–.

The inexhaustible cup. Transl. by T. D. France. 147 pp. N.Y. Dutton, 1928.

Story of a love. Transl. by N. Tsytovich. 323 pp. N.Y. Dutton, 1931.

Sun of the dead. Transl. by C. J. Hogarth. 297 pp. Ld. Dent, 1927.

That which happened. Transl. by C. J. Hogarth. Ld. 1924.

SHOLOKHOV (Mikhail Aleksandrovich), 1905–

And quiet flows the Don. Transl. by S. Garry. 755 pp. Ld. Putnam, 1934.

The Don flows home to the sea (*Silent Don*, pt. 1), with *And quiet flows the Don* (*Silent Don*, pt. 2). Transl. by S. Garry. 868 pp. Ld. Putnam, 1940.

Down south. (*In :* I. Montagu and H. Marshall, *Soviet short stories*, 1943.)

The science of hatred. (*In : Soviet war stories*, 1944.)

Seeds of tomorrow. Transl. by S. Garry. 404 pp. N.Y. Knopf, 1935.

—— Same. 404 pp. N.Y. Knopf, 1942. (Alblabooks.)

—— Same. With title: *Virgin soil upturned.* Transl. by S. Garry. 488 pp. Ld. Putnam, 1935.

—— Same. (*Extract in :* G. Reavey and M. Slonim, *Soviet literature*, 1933.)

SHOSHIN (M.).

A rendezvous. (*In :* E. Fen, *Soviet stories of the last decade*, 1945.)

SHPANOV (Nikolay).

The musician. (*In :* I. Montagu and H. Marshall, *Soviet short stories*, 1943.)

SIMONOV (Konstantin).

The cossack. (*In :* I. Montagu and H. Marshall, *Soviet short stories*, 1944.)

'Moscow'; 'On the Petsamo Road'; 'His only son'; 'The cossack song'; 'The bridge under the water'; 'Three days'; 'Paramon Samsovovich'; 'Maturity'. (*In : Soviet war stories*, 1943.)

No quarter. 231 pp. N.Y. Fischer, 1943.

The only son. (*In :* E. Fen, *Soviet stories of the last decade*, 1945.)

On the cliffs of Norway. (*In :* I. Montagu and H. Marshall, *Soviet short stories*, 1943.)

The Russians. (*In : Four Soviet war plays*, 1943.)

The third adjutant. (*In :* I. Montagu and H. Marshall, *Soviet short stories*, 1943.)

SIRIN [pseud.]. *See :* NABOKOV (Vladimir Vladimirovich).

SKITALETS [pseud. of Stepan Gavrilovich Petrov], 1868–.

The Czar's charter. Transl. by P. L. Ld. Henderson's, 1907.

Publican and serf. Transl. by J. K. M. Shirazi. Ld. Alston Rivers, 1905.

SKOBOLOV (Aleksandr Sergeevich). *See :* NEVEROV (Aleksandr) [pseud.].

SLOBODSKY (M.). *See :* RASKIN (A.) and SLOBODSKY (M.).

SMIDOVICH (Vikenty Vikentevich). *See :* VERESAEV (Vikenty) [pseud.].

SMIRNOVA (N.).

Marfa; a Siberian novel. Transl. by M. Burr. 246 pp. Ld. Boriswood, 1932.

SOBOL (Andrey Mikhailovich), 1888–1926.

Freak show. Transl. by J. Covan. 416 pp. N.Y. Kendall, 1930.

SOBOLEV (Leonid).

The blue scarf. (*In:* I. Montagu and H. Marhsall, *Soviet short stories,* 1943.)

Romanoff. Abridged version by N. M. Gubsky. Transl. by A. Fremantle. 311 pp. Ld. Longmans, 1935.

—— Same. With title: *Storm warning.* 320 pp. Ld. Dickson, 1935.

The sniper. (*In:* I. Montagu and H. Marshall, *Soviet short stories,* 1943.)

SOKOLOV (Boris Fedorovich), 1893–.

The crime of Doctor Garine. Anon. transl. With an introduction by T. Dreiser. 144 pp. N.Y. Covici, 1928. [Short stories. Contains: 'The crime of Doctor Garine'; 'Strategy'; 'In Stantzia'.]

SOKOLOV-NIKITOV (I.).

The sea breeze. (*In:* E. Fen, *Soviet stories of the last decade,* 1945.)

SOLOGUB [pseud. of Fedor Kuzmich Teternikov], 1863–1927.

The created legend. Transl. by J. Cournos. Ld. Secker, 1916. [This is only the first pt. of the work of the same name. The Russian title of this pt. is *Drops of blood.*]

The little demon. Transl. by J. Cournos and R. Aldington. Ld. Secker, 1916.

Little tales. Transl. by J. Cournos. Ld. 1917.

The old house, and other stories. Transl. by J. Cournos. Ld. Secker, 1915. [Contains: 'The old house'; 'The unitor of souls'; 'The invoker of the beast'; 'The white dog'; 'The glimmer of hunger'.]

Poems. (*In:* C. M. Bowra, *A book of Russian verse,* 1943.]

Poems. (*In:* C. F. Coxwell, *Russian poems,* 1929.)

Poems. (*In:* B. Deutsch and A. Yarmolinsky, *Russian poetry,* 1929.)

Poems. (*In:* P. Selver, *Anthology of modern Slavonic literature,* 1919.)

The sweet-scented name, and other fairy tales, fables and stories. Transl. by R. Graham, with an introduction by S. Graham. Ld. Constable, 1915. (Constable's Russian Library.) [Contains: 'The sweet-scented name'; 'Wings'; 'Turandina'; 'Lohengrin'; 'The herald of the beast'; 'Equality'; 'Adventures of a cobblestone'.]

The tiny man. (*In:* P. Selver, *Anthology of modern Slavonic literature,* 1919.)

'Turandina'; 'The herald of the beast'; 'Equality', and 'Adventures of a cobblestone', repr. in: S. Graham, *Great Russian short stories*, 1929.

SOLOVYOV (Vladimir Sergeevich), 1853–1900.

God, man and the church; the spiritual foundations of life. Transl. by D. Attwater. 192 pp. Milwaukee, Bruce Publ., 1938.

The justification of the good. Transl. by N. Duddington. Ld. Constable, 1918. (Constable's Russian Library.)

Poems. (*In:* C. M. Bowra, *A book of Russian verse*, 1943.)

Poems. (*In:* C. F. Coxwell, *Russian poems*, 1929.)

The two hermits. (*In:* S. Graham, *Great Russian short stories*, 1929.)

War and Christianity. N.Y. Putnam, 1915.

War, progress and the end of history, including a short history of Anti-Christ. Transl. by A. Bakshy. Ld. Univ. Pr., 1915.

Biography, criticism, etc.:

BAKSHY (A.): *The philosophy of Vladimir Solovyov.* Aberdeen. Univ. Pr., 1916.

D'HERBIGNY (M.): *Vladimir Solovyov: a Russian Newman.* Transl. by A. M. Buchanan. Ld. Washbourne, 1918.

STEPNIAK (Sergey) [pseud. of Sergey M. Kravchinsky], 1852–95.

The career of a nihilist: a novel. Ld. Scott, 1890; N.Y. Harper, 1907. [Written in English.]

The new convert. Transl. by T. B. Eyges. Boston. Stratford, 1917.

SURGUCHEV (Ilya Dmitrievich).

Autumn: a play in four acts. Transl. by D. A. Modell. 86 pp. N.Y. and Ld. Appleton, 1924. [Appleton's Modern Plays.)

SURIKOV (I. Z.), 1841–80.

Poems. (*In:* C. M. Bowra, *A book of Russian verse*, 1943.)

SVETLOV (Mikhail Arcadevich), 1903–.

Poems. (*In: New Directions in prose and poetry*, 1941.)

TARASOV–RODIONOV (Aleksandr Ignatevich), 1885–.

Chocolate. Transl. by C. Malamuth. 311 pp. Ld. Heinemann, 1933.

—— Same. Cheap ed. 1934.

February 1917. Transl. by W. A. Drake. 378 pp. N.Y. Covici, 1931.

TETERNIKOV (Fedor Kuzmich). *See:* SOLOGUB [pseud. of Fedor Kuzmich Teternikov.]

TIKHONOV (Nikolay Semyonovich), 1896–.

A child is born. (*In:* I. Montagu and H. Marshall, *Soviet short stories*, 1943.)

The family. (*In:* same.)

Fritz. Transl. by A. Brown. (*In:* J. Rodker, *Soviet anthology,* 1943.)

The mother. (*In:* I. Montagu and H. Marshall, *Soviet short stories,* 1943.)

The old soldier. (*In:* same.)

Poem. (*In: New Directions in prose and poetry,* p. 650, 1941.)

The Soviet writer.` (*In:* I. Montagu and H. Marshall, *Soviet short stories,* 1944.)

Story with a footnote. Transl. by S. Garry. (Penguin New Writing, 5. Ld. 1941.)

Yorgyy, and two poems from 'The horde'. (*In:* G. Reavey and M. Slonim, *Soviet literature,* 1933.)

TIKHONOV (Valentin).

Mountains and the stars: a novel. 426 pp. Ld. Heinemann, 1939.

TOLSTOY (Aleksey Konstantinovich, Count), 1817–75.

Czar Feodor Ivanovich. Transl. by A. Hayes. Ld. Kegan Paul, 1924. [Pt. 2 of a trilogy.]

—— Same. Transl. by J. Covan. (*In:* O. M. Sayler, *Moscow Art Theatre series of Russian plays,* first series, 1923.)

The death of Ivan the Terrible. Transl. by A. Hayes. Ld. Kegan Paul, 1926. [Pt. 1 of a trilogy.]

—— Same. Transl. by G. R. Noyes. (*In his: Masterpieces of the Russian drama,* 1933.)

Poems. (*In:* C. M. Bowra, *A book of Russian verse,* 1943.)

Poems. (*In:* F. Cornford and E. P. Salaman, *Poems from the Russian,* 1943.)

Poems. (*In:* C. F. Coxwell, *Russian poems,* 1929.)

A prince of outlaws. Transl. by C. A. Manning. N.Y. Knopf, 1927. [Transl. before under the title: *The terrible Czar,* 1892; and *Prince Serbryani, a historical novel,* 1892.]

TOLSTOY (Aleksey Nikolaevich), 1882–1945.

The affair on the Basseynaya street. (*In:* J. Cournos, *Short stories out of Soviet Russia,* 1929.)

Azure cities. (*In:* J. J. Robbins and J. Kunitz, *Azure cities,* 1929.)

Bread: a novel. Transl. by S. Garry. 447 pp. Ld. Gollancz, 1938.

Darkness and dawn. Transl. by E. Bone and E. Burns. 570 pp. Ld. Gollancz, 1936.

Death box. Transl. by B. G. Guerney. 357 pp. Ld. Methuen, 1937.

Imperial Majesty. Transl. by H. C. Matheson. 444 pp. Ld. Matthews & Marrot, 1932. [Vol. 1 of *Peter the Great.*]

My country; articles and stories of the Great Patriotic War of the Soviet Union. Transl. by D. L. Fromberg. 117 pp. Ld. Hutchinson, 1943.

Peter the Great. Transl. by E. Bone and E. Burns. 463 pp. Ld. Gollancz, 1936.

The road to Calvary. Transl. by R. S. Townsend. N.Y. Boni, 1923.

Smashnose. (*In:* S. Konovalov, *Bonfire*, 1932.)

Vasily Suchkov. (*Extract in:* S. Konovalov, *Bonfire*, 1932.)

The Viper. Transl. by E. Fen. (*In her: Modern Russian stories,* 1943.)

A white night. (*In:* J. Cournos, *Short stories out of Soviet Russia,* 1929.)

TOLSTOY (Ilya Lvovich).

Reminiscences of Tolstoy by his son. Transl. by G. Calderon. N.Y. Century, 1914.

TOLSTOY (Lev Nikolaevich, Count), 1828–1910.

Collected works:

The novels and other works of Lyof N. Tolstoi. Edited by N. H. Dole, translated by I. F. Hapgood, N. H. Dole and others. N.Y. Scribner, 1902. 22 vols.

    Also known as the International Edition. Reprinted in 1923 in 24 vols.

(Works) by Count Lev N. Tolstoy; translated from the original Russian and edited by Prof. Leo Wiener. Boston. Colonial Press Co., 1904–12. 14 vols. (Vols. 13 and 14 not numbered by the publisher, contain posthumous works, edited by Hagberg Wright. Vol. 14 contains 'Hadji Murad', translated by Aylmer Maude.) This edition appeared in England under the imprint of Dent.

Tolstoy Centenary edition. Edited by Aylmer Maude. Ld. For the Tolstoy Society, Oxf. Univ. Pr. (Humphrey Milford), 1928–37. 21 vols. (Translation by Louise and Aylmer Maude.)

Contents:

Vols. 1–2. *Maude: Life of Tolstoy.*

  Vol. 3. *Childhood, Boyhood and Youth.*

  Vol. 4. *Tales of army life:* 'Sevastopol in Dec. 1884, Sevastopol in May 1855, Sevastopol in August 1855'; 'The Cossacks'; 'The raid'; 'The wood-felling'; 'Meeting a Moscow acquaintance in the detachment'.

Vol. 5. *Nine stories:* 'Two Hussars'; 'A Landlord's morning'; 'Polikushka'; 'A billiard-marker's notes'; "The snow-storm'; 'Lucerne'; 'Albert'; 'Three deaths'; 'Strider, the story of a horse'.

Vols. 6–8. *War and Peace.*

Vol. 9. *Anna Karenina.*

Vol. 11. *Confession,* and *The Gospel in brief:* 'What I believe'; 'Conclusion of "A criticism of dogmatic theology"'; 'Introduction to "An examination of the Gospels"'; 'Prefaces to editions of "The four Gospels".'

Vol. 12. *On life,* and *Essays on religion:* 'What is religion?'; 'The teaching of Jesus'; 'Religion and morality'; 'Reason and religion'; 'How to read the Gospels'; 'Preface to *The Christian teaching*'; 'An appeal to the clergy'; 'A reply to the Synod's Edict of excommunication'; 'The restoration of Hell'; 'Church and state'.

Vol. 13. *Twenty-three tales:* 'God sees the truth but waits'; 'A prisoner in the Caucasus'; 'The bear hunt'; 'What men live by'; 'A spark neglected burns the house'; 'Two old men'; 'Where love is, God is'; 'Ivan the fool'; 'Evil allures but good endures'; 'Little girls wiser than men'; 'Elias'; 'The three hermits'; 'The imp and the crust'; 'How much land does a man need?'; 'A grain as big as a hen's egg'; 'The godson'; 'The repentant sinner'; 'The empty drum'; 'The coffee-house of Surat'; 'Too dear!'; 'Esarhaddon, King of Assyria'; 'Work, death and sickness'; 'Three questions'.

Vol. 14. *What then must we do?:* 'Letter to Engelhardt'.

Vol. 15. *Ivan Ilych,* and *Hadji Murad:* 'Master and man'; 'Fedor Kuzmich'; 'Memoirs of a madman'; 'Walk in the light while there is light'; 'A talk among leisured people'.

Vol. 16. *The Devil and cognate tales:* 'Family happiness'; 'The Kreutzer sonata'; 'The porcelain doll'; 'Francoise'; 'Father Sergius'.

Vol. 17. *Plays:* 'The first distiller'; 'The power of darkness'; 'The fruits of enlightenment'; 'The light shines in darkness'; 'The live corpse'; 'The cause of it all'.

Vol. 18. *What is art?* and *Essays on art:* 'On truth in art'; Introduction to 'Amiel's journal', to 'Semenov's Peasant stories', to Guy de Maupassant. Preface to 'Der Buttnerbauer'; An afterword to Chekhov's 'Darling'; 'On art'.

Vol. 19. *Resurrection.*

Vol. 20. *The kingdom of God is within you,* and *Peace essays.*

Vol. 21. *Recollections, and Essays :* 'Why do men stupefy themselves ?'; 'The first step'; 'Non-acting'; 'An afterword to Famine articles'; 'Modern science'; 'An introduction to Ruskin's works'; 'Letters on Henry George'; 'Thou shalt not kill'; 'Bethink yourselves'; 'A great iniquity'; 'Shakespeare and the drama'; 'What's to be done?'; 'I cannot be silent'; 'A letter to a Hindu'; 'Gandhi letters'; 'Letter to a Japanese'; 'The wisdom of children'; 'Thoughts from private letters'.

This ed. is also issued by the Oxf. Univ. Pr. in the World's Classics Series.

Anna Karenina. Transl. by C. Garnett. 2 vols. Ld. Heinemann, 1901.

—— Same. Transl. by R. S. Townsend. 2 vols. Ld. Dent, 1912. (Everyman's Library.)

The death of Ivan Ilyitch, and other stories. A new transl. by C. Garnett. Ld. Heinemann, 1902. [Contains : 'The death of Ivan Ilyitch'; 'Family happiness'; 'Polikushka'; 'Two hussars'; 'The snowstorm'; 'Three deaths'.]

The dominion of darkness. Transl. by L. and A. Maude. Ld. 1905.

—— Same. With title : *The power of darkness.* Transl. by G. R. Noyes and G. Z. Patrick. (*In :* G. R. Noyes, *Masterpieces of the Russian drama,* 1933.)

Living thoughts of Tolstoy. Presented by S. Zweig. 154 pp. N.Y. Longmans, 1939; Ld. Cassell, n.d.

Resurrection. Transl. by L. Maude. Ld. 1900.

—— Same. Rev. ed. Ld. 1902.

—— Same. Transl. by L. Wiener. 2 vols. Boston. Dana Estes, 1904.

—— Same. Transl. by A. J. Wolfe. 2 vols. N.Y. International Publishing Co., 1920.

Sevastopol; Two hussars, etc. Transl. by L. and A. Maude. 325 pp. Ld. Constable, 1905.

War and peace. Transl. by C. Garnett. 3 vols. Ld. Heinemann, 1904.

—— Same. Popular ed. 1911.

—— Same. Anon. transl. 3 vols. Ld. Dent, 1911. (Everyman's Library.)

—— Same. Transl. by L. and A. Maude. With an introduction. 1,352 pp. Ld. Macmillan ; Oxf. Univ. Pr., 1942. [Repr. from the Centenary ed.]

—— Same. Rev. Ill. by Verestchagin and F. Eichenberg. 2 vols. N.Y. Heritage, 1943.

Diaries: youth, 1847–1852. Transl. by C. J. Hogarth and A. Sirnis. With a preface by C. H. Wright. Ld. Dent, 1917.

The private diary of Leo Tolstoy, 1853–1857. 256 pp. N.Y. Doubleday, 1927.

The letters of Tolstoy and his cousin Countess Alexandra Tolstoy, 1857–1903. 232 pp. Ld. Methuen, 1929.

The journal of L. Tolstoy, 1895–1899. 427 pp, N.Y. Knopf, 1917.

Tolstoy. Literary fragments, letters and reminiscences. 330 pp. N.Y. Dial Pr., 1931.

Tolstoy's love-letters. Transl. by V. Woolf and S. S. Koteliansky. With a study of the autobiographical element in Tolstoy's work by P. Biryukov. 134 pp. Ld. Hogarth Pr., 1923.

Biography, criticism, etc.:

WIENER (L.): *Bibliography of works and articles on Tolstoy in Engl., German and French.* (*In: Complete works of Tolstoy.* Transl. and ed. by L. Wiener. Vol. of 1905.)

YASSUKOVICH (A.): *Tolstoy in English, 1878–1929; a list of works by and about Tolstoy available in the New York Public Library.* (*Bulletin of the New York Public Library*, vol. 33, no. 7, July 1929.)

ABRAHAM (G.): *Tolstoy.* 144 pp. Ld. Duckworth, 1935.

BARING (M.): *Tolstoy and Turgenev.* (*In his: Landmarks in Russian literature*, 1910.)

BAUDOUIN (C.): *Tolstoi: the teacher.* 218 pp. N.Y. Dutton, 1923.

BIRYUKOV (P.): *L. Tolstoy; his life and work; autobiographical memoirs, letters and biographical material.* 2 vols. N.Y. 1906.

—— Same. *The life of Tolstoy.* Transl. from the Russian. 168 pp. Ld. 1911.

CHESTERTON (G. K.) and PERRIS (G. H.) and GARNETT (E.): *Leo Tolstoy.* 40 pp. Ill. Ld. 1903. (Bookman Biographies.)

DAVIS (H. E.): *Tolstoy and Nietzsche: a problem in biographical ethics.* 271 pp. N.Y. New Republic, 1929.

DILLON (E. J.): *Count L. Tolstoy: a new portrait.* 286 pp. Ld. Hutchinson, 1934.

FAUSSET (H. l'A.): *Tolstoy, the inner drama.* 320 pp. Ld. Cape, 1927.

GARNETT (E.): *Tolstoy: his life and writings.* Ld. Constable, 1914.

GARROD (H. W.) : *Tolstoi's theory of art.* 25 pp. Oxf. Clarendon Pr., 1935. (Taylorian Lecture.)

GOLDENVEIZER (A. B.) : *Talks with Tolstoi.* 182 pp. Richmond. L. & V. Woolf, 1923.

GORKY (M.) : *Reminiscences of Leo Nikolaevich Tolstoi.* Transl. by S. S. Koteliansky and V. Woolf. 70 pp. Richmond. L. & V. Woolf, 1920.

GUTHRIE (A. L.) : *Wordsworth and Tolstoi, and other papers.* 124 pp. Edinburgh. Constable, 1922.

KNIGHT (G. W.) : *Shakespeare and Tolstoy.* 27 pp. Ld. Oxf. Univ. Pr., 1934.

KNOWLSON (T. S.) : *Leo Tolstoy : a biographical and critical study.* 190 pp. Ld. and N.Y. Warner, 1904.

KVITKO (D.) : *A philosophical study of Tolstoy.* 119 pp. N.Y. 1927.

LAVRIN (J.) : *Tolstoy : a psycho-critical study.* 223 pp. Ld. Collins, 1924.

LLOYD (J. A. T.) : *Two Russian reformers : Ivan Turgenev, Leo Tolstoy.* 325 pp. N.Y. Lane, 1911.

MANN (T.) : *Past masters, and other essays.* 275 pp. N.Y. Knopf, 1933. [Contains essay on Tolstoy.]

—— Same. *Three essays.* 261 pp. N.Y. Knopf, 1929. [Contains essay on : Goethe and Tolstoy.]

MAUDE (A.) : *Family views on Tolstoy.* Ed. by A. Maude. Transl. by L. and A. Maude. 220 pp. Ld. Allen & Unwin, 1926.

—— Same. *The life of Tolstoy : first fifty years.* 464 pp. Ld. Constable, 1908. And : *Later years.* 688 pp. Ld. Constable, 1910.

MEREZHKOVSKY (D. S.) : *Tolstoi as man and artist, with an essay on Dostoevsky.* 310 pp. N.Y. and Ld. Putnam, 1902.

NAZAROFF (A. J.) : *Tolstoy, the inconstant genius : a biography.* 332 pp. N.Y. Stokes, 1930.

NOYES (G. R.) : *Tolstoy.* 395 pp. N.Y. Duffield, 1918 ;· Ld. 1919.

ROLLAND (R.) : *Tolstoy.* Transl. from the French by B. Miall. 321 pp. Ld. 1911.

TOLSTOY (A., Countess) : *The tragedy of Tolstoy.* 294 pp. New Haven. Yale Univ. Pr., 1933.

TOLSTOY (I. L.) : *Reminiscences of Tolstoy by his son.* Transl. by G. Calderon. N.Y. Century, 1914.

—— Same. *The truth about my father.* 229 pp. N.Y. Appleton, 1927.

TOLSTOY (S. A.).   *See:* under her own works: TOLSTOY (Sophie Andreevna).

ZWEIG (S.): *Adepts in self-portraiture: Casanova, Stendhal, Tolstoy.* 357 pp. N.Y. Viking Pr., 1928.

TOLSTOY (Sophie Andreevna, Countess):
Autobiography of the Countess Sophie Tolstoy. With a preface and notes by V. Spiridonov. Transl. by S. S. Koteliansky and L. Woolf. Ld. Hogarth Pr., 1922.
The diary of Tolstoy's wife: 1860–1891. Transl. by A. Werth. 272 pp. Ld. Gollancz, 1928.
The final struggle: being Countess Tolstoy's diary for 1910, with extracts from Tolstoy's diaries. Transl. by A. Maude. 407 pp. Ld. Allen, 1936.
The later diary: 1891–1897. Transl. by A. Werth. Ld. Gollancz, 1929.

TRENYEV (Konstantin).
The birthday. (*In:* I. Montagu and H. Marshall, *Soviet short stories,* 1944.)

TRETYAKOV (Sergey Mikhailovich), 1892–.
Chinese testament. The autobiography of Tan Shih-hua as told to Tretyakov. 383 pp. Ld. Gollancz, 1934.
Roar China! an episode in nine scenes. Transl. by F. Polianovska and B. Nixon. 87 pp. Ld. Lawrence, 1931.

TSVETAEVA (Marina), 1892–.
The separation. (*In:* G. Reavey and M. Slonim, *Soviet literature,* 1933.)

TUPIKOV (Pavel Georgevich), 1882–.
Ocean. Transl. by J. Cournos. 421 pp. Ld. Hamilton, 1936.

TURGENEV (Ivan Sergeevich), 1818–83.
The novels and tales. Transl. by Constance Garnett. Ld. Heinemann, 1894–99. 15 vols.
—— Library ed., 1919–1923. 17 vols.
Contents:
Vol. 1. *Rudin.*
Vol. 2. *A house of gentlefolk.*
Vol. 3. *On the eve.*
Vol. 4. *Fathers and children.*
Vol. 5. *Smoke.*
Vols. 6–7. *Virgin soil.*
Vols. 8–9. *Sportsman's sketches.*
Vol. 10. *Dream tales and prose poems:* 'Clara Militch'; 'Phantoms'; 'The song of triumphant love'; 'The dream'; 'Poems in prose'.

Vol. 11. 'Torrents of Spring'; 'First Love'; 'Mumu'.

Vol. 12. *A Lear of the Steppes*, etc.

Vol. 13. 'Diary of a superfluous man'; 'A tour in the forest'; 'Yakov Pasinkov'; 'Andrei Kolosov'; 'A correspondence'.

Vol. 14. 'A desperate character'; 'A strange story'; 'Punin and Baburin'; 'Old portraits'; 'The brigadier'; 'Pyetushkov'.

Vol. 15. 'The Jew'; 'An unhappy girl'; 'The duellist'; 'Three portraits'; 'Enough'.

Vol. 16. *The two friends, and other stories.*

Vol. 17. *Knock, knock, knock, etc.*

Novels and tales. Translated by I. F. Hapgood. N.Y. Scribner, 1903. 13 vols.

The plays of Ivan S. Turgenev. Transl. by M. S. Mandell. N.Y. Macmillan; Ld. Heinemann, 1924.

Contents: 'Carelessness'; 'Broke'; 'Where it is thin, there it breaks'; 'The family charge'; 'The bachelor'; 'An amicable settlement'; 'A month in the country'; 'The country woman'; 'A conversation on the highway'; 'An evening in Sorrento'.

Three plays. Transl. by Constance Garnett. Ld. Cassell, 1934. [*Contains:* 'A month in the country'; 'A provincial lady'; 'A poor gentleman'.]

Asya. [Formerly transl. under the title: *Annouchka.*] Transl. by A. E. Chamot. (*In his: Selected Russian short stories*, 1925.)

Fathers and sons. Transl. by C. J. Hogarth. 276 pp. Ld. Dent, 1921. (Everyman's Library.)

Hamlet and Don Quixote. Transl. by R. Nichols. 88 pp. Ld. Henderson's, 1930.

A house of gentlefolk. [Formerly transl. under the title: *Liza.*] Transl. by I. F. Hapgood. N.Y. 1903.

—— Same. With title: *A nest of hereditary legislators.* Done into Engl. by F. Davies. Ld. Simkin & Marshall, 1914.

A month in the country. Transl. by G. R. Noyes. (*In his: Masterpieces of the Russian drama*, 1933.)

—— Same. *A comedy.* Adapted into Engl. by E. Williams 93 pp. Ld. Heinemann, 1943.

Poems. (*In:* C. F. Coxwell, *Russian poems*, 1929.)

Biography, criticism, etc.:

OSBOURNE (E. A.): *Russian literature and translation. 6. Ivan S. Turgenev.* (*Bookman*, vol. 83. Ld. 1932.)

BARING (M.): *The place of Turgenev*, and: *Tolstoy and Turgenev.* (*In his: Landmarks in Russian literature*, 1910.)

GARNETT (E. W.): *Turgenev: a study.* Ld. Collins, 1917.

GETTMANN (R. A.): *Turgenev in England and America.* 196 pp. Urbana, 1941. (*Illinois studies in language and literature,* Vol. 27, No. 2.)

HERSHKOWITZ (H.): *Democratic ideas in Turgenev's works.* Columbia, 1932.

LLOYD (J. A. T.): *Ivan Turgenev: a literary biography.* Ld. Hale, 1943.

—— Same. *Two Russian reformers: I. Turgenev, L. Tolstoy.* 325 pp. N.Y. Lane, 1911.

YARMOLINSKY (A.): *Turgenev: the man, his art and his age.* 386 pp. N.Y. Century, 1926; Ld. Hodder & Stoughton, 1927.

TYNYANOV (Yuri Nikolaevich), 1894–.
Death and diplomacy in Persia. Transl. by A. Brown. 357 pp. Ld. Boriswood, 1938. [Historical novel on the life of the author A. S. Griboedov.]
Second Lieutenant Also. (*In:* I. Montagu and H. Marshall, *Soviet short stories,* 1942.)

TYUCHEV (Fedor Ivanovich), 1803–73.
Poem. (*In:* O. Elton, *Verse from Pushkin and others,* 1935.)
Poems. (*In:* C. M. Bowra, *A book of Russian verse,* 1943.)
Poems. (*In:* F. Cornford and E. P. Salaman, *Poems from the Russian,* 1943.)
Poems. (*In:* C. F. Coxwell, *Russian poems,* 1929.)
Poems. (*In:* N. Jarintzov, *Russian poets and poems,* 1917.)

UKRAINKA (Lesya) [pseud. of Larissa Petrovna Kossatch], 1872–1913.
The Babylonian captivity. (*In:* C. E. Bechhofer, *Five Russian plays,* 1916.)

USHAKOV (Nikolay), 1899–.
Karabash. (*In:* G. Reavey and M. Slonim, *Soviet literature,* 1933.)

USPENSKIY (Andrey Vasilevich). *See:* KIRSHON (V. M.) and USPENSKIY (A. V.).

VERESAEV (Vikenty) [pseud. of Vikenty Vikentevich Smidovich], 1867–.
The confessions of a physician. Transl. by A. S. Linden. Ld. Grant Richards, 1904.
The deadlock. Transl. by N. Vissotsky and C. Coventry. 352 pp. Ld. Faber, 1927.
The sisters. Transl. by J. Soskice. 288 pp. Ld. Hutchinson, 1934.

VESELY (Artem) [pseud. of Nikolay Kochkurov], 1899–.
Russia drenched in blood. (*In:* S. Konovalov, *Bonfire,* 1932.)

VILENKIN (Nikolay). *See:* MINSKY (N. M.) [pseud. of Nikolay Vilenkin.].

VINOGRADOV (Anatoly Kornelevich), 1888–.
The black consul. Transl. by E. Burns. 438 pp. Ld. Gollancz, 1935.

VIRTA (Nikolay).
The root of life. Transl. by S. Garry. (*In:* J. Rodker, *Soviet anthology*, 1943.)

VISHNEVSKY (Vsevolod Vitalevich), 1900–.
An optimistic tragedy: a play in three acts. Transl. by H. G. Scott and R. S. Carr. [*In:* B. Blake, *Four Soviet plays*, 1937.)

VOGAU (Boris Andreevich). *See:* PILNYAK (Boris) [pseud. of Boris Andreevich Vogau].

VOINOVA (Aleksandra Ivanovna).
Semi-precious stones. Transl. by V. Snow. 604 pp. Ld. Cape, 1931.
—— Same. 531 pp. Ld. Heinemann, 1934.

VOITEKHOV (Boris Ilich), 1913–.
Last days of Sevastopol. Transl. by R. Parker and V. M. Genne. 224 pp. N.Y. Knopf, 1943; 150 pp. Ld. Cassell, 1943.

VOLKOV (Mikhail), 1886–.
The miracle. [Short story.] (*In:* J. J. Robbins and J. Kunitz, *Azure cities*, 1929.)

VOLOSHIN (Maksimilian Aleksandrovich), 1877–.
Poems. (*In:* C. F. Coxwell, *Russian poems*, 1929.)
Poems. (*In:* B. Deutsch and A. Yarmolinsky, *Russian poetry*, 1929.)
Poems of Russia. (*In:* G. Reavey and M. Slonim, *Soviet literature*, 1933.)

VOLOSOV (Mark).
Six rats. Transl. by A .Brown. (*In:* J. Rodker, *Soviet anthology*, 1943.)

VORONSKY (Aleksandr Konstantinovich), 1884–.
Waters of life and death. Transl. by L. Zarine. 343 pp. Ld. Allen & Unwin, 1936.

WASSILEWSKA (Wanda), 1905–.
'The commonwealth of nations'; 'Children'; 'The iron cross'. (*In: Soviet war stories*, 1943.)
Inside the hut. (*In:* I. Montagu and H. Marshall, *Soviet short stories*, 1943.)
The party cards. (*In:* I. Montagu and H. Marshall, *Soviet short stories*, 1943.)

Rainbow ; the story of a Ukrainian village under German occupation.
Transl. by E. Bone. 184 pp. Ld. Hutchinson, 1943;
American ed. transl. by S. Bleeker. 230 pp. N.Y. Simon &
Schuster, 1944. [Stalin prize novel, 1943.]

WEISSENBERG (Leo).
The alarm clock. (*In:* J. Rodker, *Soviet anthology*, 1943.)

YAKOVLEV (Aleksandr).
The Chinese vase. (*In:* S. Konovalov, *Bonfire*, 1932.)

YAZYKOV (Nikolay Mikhailovich), 1803–46.
Poems. (*In:* C. F. Coxwell, *Russian poems*, 1929.)
Poems. (*In:* P. E. Matheson, *Holy Russia*, 1918.)
Poems. (*In:* L. Wiener, *Anthology of Russian literature*, 1902.)

ZAITSEV (Boris Konstantinovich), 1881–.
Anna. Transl. by N. Duddington. 156 pp. Ld. Allen, 1937.

ZAMYATIN (Evgeny Ivanovich), 1884–1937.
Mamai. (*In:* G. Reavey and M. Slonim, *Soviet literature*, 1933.)
We. Transl. by G. Zilboorg. 286 pp. N.Y. Dutton, 1924.

ZAYAITSKY (S.).
The forgotten night. (*In:* S. Konovalov, *Bonfire*, 1932.)

ZHABOTINSKY (Vladimir Evgenevich), 1880–1940.
Judge and fool. Transl. from the German by C. Brooks. 348 pp.
N.Y. Liveright, 1930.
Samson the Nazarite. Transl. by C. Brooks. 314 pp. Ld.
Secker, 1930.

ZHAROV (Aleksandr Alekseevich), 1904–.
Poems. (*In: New Directions in prose and poetry*, 1941.)

ZHUKOVSKY (Vasily Andreevich), 1783–1852.
Poem. (*In:* P. E. Matheson, *Holy Russia*, 1918.)
Poems. (*In:* C. F. Coxwell, *Russian poems*, 1929.)
The three girdles. Transl. by L. Zarine. (*In:* S. Graham, *Great
Russian short stories*, 1929.)

ZOSHCHENKO (Mikhail Mikhailovich), 1895–.
A damp business. (*In:* S. Konovalov, *Bonfire*, 1932.)
Dawn of a new day. (*In:* I. Montagu and H. Marshall, *Soviet
short stories*, 1942.)
For children. Transl. by M. Budberg. (*In:* J. Rodker, *Soviet
anthology*, 1943.)
Gold teeth. [*Short story.*] (*In:* J. J. Robbins and J. Kunitz,
Azure cities, 1929.)
A great king's love. Transl. by A. Fremantle. (*In:* J. Rodker,
Soviet anthology, 1943.)
A hasty affair. (*In:* S. Konovalov, *Bonfire*, 1932.)
The illiterate woman. (*In:* J. Rodker, *Soviet anthology*, 1943.)

A mistake. (*In:* G. Reavey and M. Slonim, *Soviet literature,* 1933.)

Nero and his mother. (*In:* J. Rodker, *Soviet anthology,* 1943.)

The night of horror. (*In:* S. Konovalov, *Bonfire,* 1932.)

The old rat. (*In:* S. Graham, *Great Russian short stories,* 1929.)

Russia laughs. [Short stories.] Transl. by H. Clayton. 352 pp. Toronto. Longmans, 1935.

A story of adventure. (*In:* S. Konovalov, *Bonfire,* 1932.)

What the nightingale sang of. (*In:* E. Fen, *Modern Russian stories,* 1943.)

The woman who could not read, and other tales. Transl. by E. Fen. 153 pp. Ld. Methuen, 1940.

The wonderful dog, and other tales. Transl. by E. Fen. 180 pp. Ld. Methuen, 1942.

ZOZULYA (Efim), 1891–.

The mother, and *A tale about Ak and humanity.* (*In:* J. Cournos, *Short stories out of Soviet Russia,* 1929.)

V. LINGUISTIC APPENDIX

I. DICTIONARIES

ALEXÁNDROV (A.): *Complete English-Russian, Russian-English dictionary.* 5th ed. 2 vols. St. Petersburg and Ld. 1915; Milwaukee. Caspar, 1918.

BOYANUS (S. K.) and MÜLLER (V. K.): *Russian-English dictionary.* Moscow. 1932; New ed. 800 pp. N.Y. Four Continent Book Corp. 1937. (New orthography.)

—— *English-Russian dictionary.* 1,466 pp. N.Y. Bookniga, 1935.

CURRALL (R. T.): *Russian pronouncing vocabulary.* 160 pp. Ld. Harrap. 1942.

FREESE (J. H.): *Russian-English, English-Russian dictionary.* 2 vols. N.Y. Stechert, 1917.

GOLOVINSKY (M.): *The new English-Russian and Russian-English dictionary.* Milwaukee. Caspar, 1920.

Hossfeld's new pocket dictionary of the English and Russian languages. 464, 396 pp. Ld. 1906.

MILLER (A. D.) and MIRSKY (D. S.): *English-Russian dictionary.* 552 pp. N.Y. Bookniga, 1936.

MUELLER (V. K.): *English-Russian dictionary, with the addition of short grammatical rules. With Russian-English dictionary.* New ed. 776 pp. N.Y. Dutton, 1944. [Based on Boyanus and Müller, see above.]

—— *Russian-English dictionary.* 3rd ed. 822 pp. Ld. Lawrence, 1943. With English-Russian dictionary.

—— —— Same. 3rd ed. rev. 822 pp. N.Y. Dutton, 1944.

O'BRIEN (M. A.): *New English-Russian, Russian-English dictionary.* 2 vols. 363, 344 pp. Ld. Allen, 1942.

—— —— Same. In 1 vol. Ld. Allen, 1942; new ed. N.Y. Dove Publ., 1944.

ROTHSTEIN (N. F.): *New Russian-English dictionary.* 346 pp. Ld. 1944.

SCHAPIRO (W.): *Russian-English, English-Russian pocket dictionary.* 384 pp. Ld. Harrap, 1939.

SEGAL (L.): *New complete Russian-English dictionary.* 2nd ed. 965 pp. Ld. Lund Humphries, 1944.

ZAIMOVSKIY (S. G.): *English-Russian dictionary.* 1,086 pp. Milwaukee. Caspar, c. 1932.

2. GRAMMARS, ETC.

BIRKETT (G. A.): *A modern Russian course.* 330 pp. Ld. Methuen, 1937.

BISKE (R.): *Russian handwriting.* Ld. Jaschke, 1919.

BONDAR (D.): *Bondar's simplified Russian method, conversational and commercial.* 6th ed. rev. by L. Segal. 325 pp. Ld. Pitman, 1942.

BOTELHO (F. M.): *What you want to say and how to say it in Russian.* 128 pp. Philadelphia. Macrae Smith, c. 1943.

BOYANUS (S. K.): *A manual of Russian pronunciation.* 123 pp. Ld. Sidgwick & Jackson, 1935.

BOYANUS (S. K.) and JOPSON (N. B.): *Spoken Russian; a practical course.* Written and spoken colloquial Russian with pronunciation, intonation, grammar, English translation and vocabulary. (Illustrated by 12 H.M.V. records.) 366 pp. Ld. Sidgwick & Jackson, 1939.

DAVIS (I.): *The motherland; a book for the study of the Russian language.* 2 vols. Riga, 1915–16.

DUFF (C.) and KROUGLIAKOFF (A. M.): *The basis and essentials of Russian.* Published for the Orthological Institute. 215 pp. N.Y. Nelson, 1936.

FORBES (N.): *Elementary Russian grammar, with exercises.* 184 pp. Oxf. Clarendon Pr., 1919.

—— *Russian grammar.* 2nd ed. 276 pp. Oxf. Clarendon Pr., 1916.

—— *First Russian book: a practical manual of Russian declensions.* 2nd ed. 224 pp. Oxf. Clarendon Pr., 1919.

—— *Second Russian book: a practical manual of Russian verbs.* 2nd ed. 336 pp. Oxf. Clarendon Pr., 1917.

—— *Third Russian book. See under:* BILINGUAL PUBLICATIONS AND READERS.

—— *Fourth Russian book: Exercises on first and second books.* 122 pp. Oxf. Clarendon Pr., 1918.

FOURMAN (M.): *Teach yourself Russian.* 276 pp. Ld. Hodder & Stoughton, 1943. (E.U.P. Teach yourself books.)

JARINTZOV (N.): *The Russians and their language, with an introduction discussing the problems of pronunciation and transliteration.* 2nd ed. 230 pp. Oxf. Blackwell, 1916.

KANY (C. E.) and KAUN (A. S.) : *Elementary Russian conversation.*
76 pp. Boston. Heath, c. 1943.
—— *Intermediate Russian conversation.* 103 pp. N.Y. Heath,
1944. (Heath modern language series.)
KOLNI-BALOZKY (J.) : *A progressive Russian grammar.* Complete
ed. 477 pp. Ld. Pitman, 1938.
PATRICK (G. Z.) : *One thousand commonly used Russian words,
with illustrative sentences.* 107 pp. Institute of Pacific
Relations, 1935.
—— *Roots of the Russian language; an elementary guide to
Russian word-building.* 239 pp. Ld. Pitman, 1938.
SEGAL (L.) : *Russian grammar and self-educator.* 8th ed. 223 pp.
N.Y. Stechert ; Ld. Lund, 1943.
—— *Russian idioms and phrases.* 4th ed. 52 pp. Ld. Pitman,
1943.
—— *Say it in Russian: English-Russian word and phrase book
with pronunciation.* 100 pp. Southport. Zeltser, 1942;
Transatlantic, 1943.
SEMEONOFF (A. H.) : *Brush up your Russian.* (Forty up-to-date
conversations in everyday Russian, with a supplement of useful
information and practical vocabularies.) 161 pp. Ld. Dent,
1933.
—— *A new Russian grammar.* 4th ed. 322 pp. Ld. Dent,
1933.
SIEFF (M.) : *Colloquial Russian.* 323 pp. Ld. Routledge, 1943.
(Trubner's colloquial manuals.)
—— *Practical guide to the Russian accent.* 214 pp. Ld. Jaschke,
1918.
SMIRNITSKII (A. I.) : and others : *Russian for English-speaking
workers ; first year course.* Ed. by L. I. Basilevich. 332 pp.
N.Y. Amkniga, 1933.
SMIRNITSKII (A. I.) and SVESHNIKOV (P. P.) : *Russian textbook:
elementary course.* Ill. 363 pp. Ld. Lawrence, 1935. [2nd
ed. of above.]
SOMMER (F. E.) : *Essentials of modern Russian.* 64 pp. N.Y.
Ungar, c. 1943.
TROFIMOV (M. V.) and JONES (D.) : *The pronunciation of Russian.*
Ld. Cambridge Univ. Pr., 1923. (Cambridge Primers of
Pronunciation.)
UNDERWOOD (E. G.) : *Russian accentuation.* 71 pp. Edinburgh.
Blackie, 1918.
WHITFIELD (F. J.) : *Russian reference grammar.* 222 pp. Cambr.
Mass. Harvard Univ. Pr., 1944.

WILLIAMS (A. M.) : *Russian made easy : a practical introduction to the language.* 40 pp. Ld. Muller, 1943 ; N.Y. Transatlantic, 1944.

3. BILINGUAL PUBLICATIONS AND READERS

AKSAKOV (S. T.) *in* : FORBES (N.), *Third Russian book.* 1925.

BOYER (P.) and SPERANSKII (N.) : *Russian reader. Accented texts. grammatical and explanatory notes, vocabulary.* Adapted for English-speaking students by S. V. Harper. 386 pp. Chicago. Univ. of Chicago Pr., 1915.

CHEKHOV (A. P.) : *The album, and five other tales.* Ed. with introduction, notes and vocabulary by L. Segal. 2nd ed. 60 pp. Ld. Pitman, 1938.

—— *Selections of humorous stories.* Ed. by D. Bondar. 82 pp. Ld. Pitman, 1943. (Bondar's Russian Reader, 2.)

—— *Stories.* Ed. by A. S. Kaun and O. Maslenikov. 59 pp. Univ. of California, 1943. (Advanced Russian Reader, 1.)

DUDDINGTON (N. A.) : *First Russian reader.* 160 pp. Ld. Harrap, 1943.

FEN (E.) : *A beginner's Russian reader.* 35 pp. Ld. Methuen, 1942.

FORBES (N.) : *Third Russian book ; extracts from Aksakov, Grigorovich, Hertsen, Saltykov.* Accented and ed. with full notes. 204 pp. Oxf. Clarendon Pr., 1917. [Repr. 1925.]

—— *Word-for-word Russian story book.* With interlinear phonetic transcription. 55 pp. Oxf. Blackwell, 1916.

GOGOL (N. V.) : *The greatcoat.* With Engl. transl. by Z. Shoenberg and J. Domb. 56 pp. Ld. Harrap, 1944. (Harrap's bilingual series.)

GRIGOROVICH (D. V.) *in* : FORBES (N.), *Third Russian book.* 1925.

HERTSEN (A. I.) *in* : FORBES (N.), *Third Russian book.* 1925.

PATRICK (G. Z.) : *Elementary Russian reader.* 159 pp. Ld. Pitman, 1938.

—— *Advanced Russian reader.* 262 pp. Ld. Pitman, 1938.

PUSHKIN (A. S.) : *The captain's daughter.* Russian reader ed. with notes, by A. H. Semeonoff. 188 pp. Ld. Dent, 1937 ; N.Y. Dutton, 1938.

PUSHKIN (A. S.) : *The Queen of Spades.* Ed. by D. Bondar. 2nd ed. 82 pp. Ld. Pitman, 1938. (Bondar's Russian reader, 1.)

—— —— 3rd ed. 77 pp. 1943.

—— *Three tales;* 'The snowstorm'; 'The postmaster'; 'The undertaker'. Transl. by R. T. Currall. Russian text accented by A. H. Semeonoff. 56 pp. Ld. Harrap, 1919, 1929 and 1942. (Harrap's bilingual series.)

SALTYKOV (M. E.) *in* : FORBES (N.), *Third Russian book.* 1925.

SEGAL (L.) : *Russian reader.* 94 pp. Ld. Lund, 1943. (Humphreys' modern language readers.)

—— *A second Russian reader.* Ed. with vocabularies. New series. Ld. 1939.

SEMEONOFF (A. H.) : *First Russian reader, with notes and vocabulary.* 118 pp. Ld. Dent, 1935.

TILLYARD (H. J. W.) and HOPFEN (B.) : *Nelson's simplified Russian reader.* 140 pp. Ld. and Edinburgh. Nelson, 1917.

TILLYARD (H. J. W.) and SEMEONOFF (A. H.) : *Russian poetry reader.* Ed. with introduction, notes and vocabulary. Ld. 1917. (Kegan Paul's Russian texts.)

TOLSTOY (L. N.) : *A first Russian reader from L. N. Tolstoy.* With English notes and a vocabulary by P. Dearmer and V. A. Tananevich. 80 pp. Oxf. Clarendon Pr., 1917.

—— *First Russian reader, tales from L. N. Tolstoy.* Ed. with transl. of text by L. Segal. Ld. British Russian Gazette and Trade Outlook. n.d.

—— *Two tales;* 'What men live by'; 'Put out the fire before it spreads'. Transl. by R. T. Currall. Russian text accented by A. H. Semeonoff. 63 pp. Ld. Harrap, 1920, 1935 and 1942. (Harrap's bilingual series.)